Nature Guides

SEASHORE LIFE
OF INDIA

Nature Guides

SEASHORE LIFE
OF INDIA

B. F. CHHAPGAR

Published for
WORLD WIDE FUND FOR NATURE—INDIA

OXFORD UNIVERSITY PRESS
MUMBAI DELHI CALCUTTA CHENNAI

Oxford University Press, Great Clarendon Street, Oxford OX2 6DP

OXFORD NEW YORK
ATHENS AUCKLAND BANGKOK CALCUTTA
CAPE TOWN CHENNAI DAR ES SALAAM DELHI
FLORENCE HONG KONG ISTANBUL KARACHI
KUALA LUMPUR MADRID MELBOURNE MEXICO CITY
MUMBAI NAIROBI PARIS SINGAPORE
TAIPEI TOKYO TORONTO
and associates in
BERLIN IBADAN

ISBN 0 19 562857 8

Reprinted 1997

Illustrations and cover design by
P.S. Shirbavikar

PRINTED AT MULTI VISTA GLOBAL LTD, CHENNAI 600 042
AND PUBLISHED BY MANZAR KHAN,
OXFORD UNIVERSITY PRESS, 219, ANNA SALAI, CHENNAI 600 006

ACKNOWLEDGEMENT

The World Wide Fund for Nature – India are grateful to Tata Tea Limited for financial assistance in the publication of this book.

CONTENTS

FOREWORD

Life began in the oceans. From the waters the first primitive amphibians crawled on to the beaches in search, perhaps, of more sunshine, or maybe to escape the predators in the seas. They soon adapted themselves to their dual existence. Some became landlubbers who would only occasionally return to the waters for recreation, perhaps to cool themselves from the heat of the primordial sun. Life ashore has evolved ever since. The brief margin where the high tide washes the edge of the beach has been a wonderland for every child, where, like Alice, they may imagine the Walrus and the Carpenter promenading hand in hand, gathering oysters, and talking about everything from cabbages to kings! Most of us built the castles of our early ambitions on the seashore, and also saw them washed away by the eternal tides. We chased scuttler crabs into their myriad holes on the beach, we were curious about the transparent jellyfish washed ashore, we collected innumerable varieties of cowries and shells, and watched the advancing and receding tides bring up or take away with them starfish and fry, flotsam and jetsam and the occasional bottle maybe with a message in it (for us?).

This book, the sixth by Dr Chhapgar and the second to be published by World Wide Fund for Nature—India, opens to us the beautiful, everyday, yet mysterious world of the seashore. For many of us it will be a nostalgic trip back to our early days when we learnt about life as we holidayed near the sea. I hope you will read it with relish. A happy seaside holiday to you! But do remember not to pollute or litter the beach with your picnic throwaways. Take the litter away with you so that life on the seashore remains unharmed for the entertainment and education of the generations which will come after you.

Bombay
24 December 1990

Vice Admiral M. P. AWATI
P.V.S.M., Vr C (Retd.)
Chairman
World Wide Fund for Nature—India
Maharashtra State & Goa Committee

PREFACE

In the sea is to be found a variety of life far unlike that on land—an aggregation of creatures some of which are so unique that we cannot believe in their existence unless we have seen them ourselves. Observing this quaint life is like travelling to a strange country, where we need a tourist guide to help us. The function of this book is to serve as a guide to the seashore, not only to enable us to identify the more commonly occurring animals which one may chance to pick up, but also to have an idea of their peculiar habits.

Why only the seashore? The seashore is the meeting place of sea and land. And I have restricted myself to this region for three reasons. First, while sailors, fishermen and oceanographers have ample opportunities to go to sea, most persons can see and handle the inhabitants of the sea on the seashore alone. Secondly, the population of animals and plants is the richest in this region, dwindling as we go further into the sea. Thirdly, the unique variations of temperature, saltiness and desiccation have led to a diversity of life that cannot be matched elsewhere.

The scope of this book has perforce to be limited. In a country as vast as ours, with a coastline extending along 5600 kilometres, it is just not possible to have even an exhaustive *list* of all the forms of life to be found on our shores (many of which are still undiscovered). For the serious researcher, there exist numerous reports scattered in a variety of scientific journals, but most of these are inaccessible to the average student of sea life, or involve time-consuming search through specialized libraries.

There are excellent guides to the seashore life of many countries but unfortunately in India the need for such a book has somehow been overlooked so far. The present guide is an attempt to fill this lacuna. It has been the author's endeavour to present the way of life of seashore animals in a concise form, at the same time avoiding the highly technical and sometimes bombastic jargon found in 'scientific' literature. If this book succeeds in opening the eyes of young people to the mystifying beauty of life on our seashores, and in whetting their appetite to know 'why' and 'how', the author's efforts will have been amply repaid.

B. F. CHHAPGAR

INTRODUCTION

The world is full of beautiful sights and wonderful creatures, and some of the most beautiful and wonderful occur in the sea. The seashore, or more specifically the inter-tidal zone (i.e. the zone between low and high tides, exposed at ebb tide but submerged at high tide) is the most popular of all the regions of the sea, not only because of its easy accessibility, but also because of its great diversity of habitat and wildlife. The seashore is a linear interface between land and sea with its wildlife confined to a ribbon-like strip only a few hundred metres wide.

Since it is not possible to give descriptive accounts—or even the names only—of all the thousands of animals living on our shores, only common or representative animals will be found in this book. Only those which can be easily seen by the naked eye are included, so that this leaves out the exquisitely designed diatoms and Protozoa, and the wheel animalcules (Rotifera).

WHEN TO COLLECT

Unlike some of the tideless seas like the Mediterranean, the seas that lap Indian shores have tides which may range from a fraction of a metre to the prodigious 6½ metres as in the Gulf of Cambay. For example, Bombay has an average neap tidal range of 1.4 metres, and a total average tidal range of 2.5 metres. Tides in our country are predominantly semidiurnal, i.e. there are two high tides and two ebb tides in 24 hours. Both high and low tides occur roughly fifty minutes later each day. At new moon and full moon, the sea-water rises unusually high and recedes unusually low; these are called spring tides. During the first and last quarters of the moon we have neap tides, when the sea-water neither comes up very high nor recedes very low. Obviously, it is preferable to visit the seashore at the time of spring low tides, when the maximum portion of the shore is exposed. (Figure 1.)

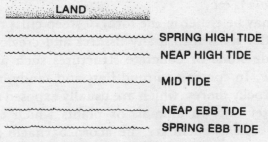

Figure 1. Water-line at different tides

1

On our shores the monsoon is so vigorous that a good part of our shore life in the inter-tidal region gets washed away or dies due to the lowering of salinity (salt-content of sea-water) due to dilution by rain-water. It is futile to seek a variety of shore life in this season. On the cessation of the rainy season, marine life starts to colonize the inter-tidal region and grows to maximum abundance in winter. After mid-February, the increasing warmth starts to affect shore life, so that it starts to decline, and is washed off once again in the rainy season. The best time of the year for observing and collecting inter-tidal life is, therefore, during winter, preferably late winter.

WHERE TO COLLECT

The animals and plants on the seashore are not distributed haphazardly; each kind occupies a well-defined zone. What we find on the seashore will depend not only on the state of the tide but also on the type of shore. Seashores can be roughly classified into rocky, shingle, sandy and muddy.

Shingle, or pebble, beaches are covered by smoothly rounded stones. These cannot retain water between them, and waves constantly roll them about so that life cannot settle on them. Shingle beaches are therefore barren and not worth collecting on.

Sandy beaches are exposed to surf (waves). These waves lift the upper layers of sand in a cloud of abrasive particles; this scouring action is harmful to life and only those forms which can take refuge by burrowing can survive. A sandy beach therefore looks apparently barren until one starts digging. We can then find typical sand-dwelling animals like the ghost crab (*Ocypode*), mole crab (*Emerita*), cockle (*Cardita*), razor shell (*Solen*) and wedge clam (*Donax*), among others.

Mud consists of very fine particles, which can accumulate only where there is restricted wave action. The fine size of mud particles enables easy burrowing and also prevents drying up of mud even at the surface. Typical mud dwellers are the sea anemone (*Paracondylactis*), *Corymorpha*, tapestry clam (*Paphia*), lugworm (*Arenicola*), etc.

Rocky shores may be either in the form of steep cliffs running down into the sea or extensive flat slabs with many fissures and crevices. Here we may also include man-made stone or concrete structures such as marinas and wharf piles, for example. In contrast to mud flats and sandy beaches, which can be easily burrowed, rocky shores, which are usually exposed to strong wave action, can provide shelter only to animals or plants which can cling to the rock surface. Typical rock dwellers are the acorn barnacle (*Balanus*), periwinkle (*Littorina*), oyster (*Ostrea*), mussel (*Perna*), hydroids (*Obelia*), bryozoa

2

(*Membranipora*), rock sea anemones, and seaweeds such as *Ulva*, *Enteromorpha*, *Padina*, and so on.

On flat rocky shores we have the limpet (*Cellana*), the sea hare (*Aplysia*), many gastropod snails and most types of seaweeds. A large variety of life-forms intolerant to desiccation, like fishes, octopi, and sea slugs, are found in rock pools which retain some water even at ebb tide.

Although we have classified the seashore into rocky, sandy and muddy, we may also have mixed shores, having two or all three components. Thus a sandy beach may open into mud flats at a lower level, and also have rounded stones or boulders on it. Such places provide ideal collecting sites as they have all the three components of a shore.

At some places in India, for example in the Gulf of Kachchh (Port Okha, Pirotan Island), on the south-eastern coast near Rameswaram, and on the Lakshadweep Islands, and Andaman and Nicobar Islands, we have extensive coral reefs. Corals are living animals related to sea anemones which secrete an external skeleton of lime. This, after their death, serves as a hard substrate, a substitute rock, on or in which many animals and plants live.

Marshes, occurring in patches in many of our creeks and estuaries, and in vast areas like the Sundarbans of Bengal, are typically inhabited by the mangroves—terrestrial trees which have secondarily invaded the sea, very successfully.

HOW TO COLLECT

On rocky faces, since most of the animals and plants live attached to the surface, they can be easily seen and picked up. However, quite a lot of animals lie hidden between the fronds of seaweeds. In rock pools, on sandy beaches and mud flats, what is visible at first glance is but a small fraction of the total population, as much of it lives under stones, or burrows into the ground.

Most of the animals in a rock pool can be collected by turning over stones. While this will disturb the animals so that the active fishes and prawns will swim away to hide in cracks, and the crabs will scuttle away, you can see the slowly wriggling brittle stars and worms, or a contracting sea anemone. Remember always to turn the stone back to its original position, so that the sessile (immobile) animals such as sponges, sea anemones, tube-dwelling worms, hydroids and bryozoa are not exposed to the sun's heat or to their enemies. Brittle stars, many worms and some sea slugs are very sensitive to handling, and may break into pieces in your hands; gently slide them into a glass bottle or polythene bag containing sea-water.

Animals on rock faces will require to be scraped off with some force; an old chisel or scalpel is ideal for the purpose. Limpets should be suddenly wrenched off while they are relaxed; once they are disturbed and on their guard it is very difficult to prise them off.

Burrowing animals can be dug out with a shovel or small rake.

Conservation of wildlife in the sea is as important as on land. Be content to watch the seashore life intently. If you must collect, do not overdo it. One specimen of each kind, if required as a museum specimen, may be taken away, but no more. If you desire to study it alive, remember that most people do not have the expertise to be able to maintain marine animals alive for more than a day or two. It is best to return the animals to the seashore near the place where you collected them. It is only an inconsiderate batch of students who go rampaging about the seashore, overturning each and every stone they come across, not bothering to return it to its original position, and collecting vast numbers of each and every form of life they come across, only to throw them in the dustbin at the end of the day. Do not be one of them.

A rectangular hand-net is suitable for catching fishes, or even large crabs if you are worried about their claws nipping your fingers. Animals with sharp spines, like sea urchins, spider crabs and lobsters should be handled with care. Blunt-tipped forceps (tongs) are ideal for lifting up delicate and soft animals like worms and sea slugs. Remember that many animals are venomous or can sting. Some of the hydroid colonies and jellyfish sting badly, and spines of fishes like the sting ray, scorpion fish or catfish and of some sea urchins also contain venom. Any cuts or wounds should be immediately bathed with clean water and an antiseptic applied on them.

The animals can be placed in polythene bags or glass bottles, and larger ones in plastic buckets. Small and delicate animals such as sea slugs are best kept in small vials. It is almost impossible to search for minute forms such as sea spiders, skeleton shrimps, amphipods and some worms directly on the seashore. It is best to bring back a colony of hydroids, bryozoa, seaweeds or sponges and keep them in an enamel or glass tray or jar overnight. By the next day the lack of oxygen in the water will force these tiny animals to drop to the bottom from where they can be picked up.

Animals can be preserved in four per cent formaline, prepared by diluting one part of commercial formaldehyde with nine parts of sea-water. Or they may be washed with tap-water and preserved in 70 per cent alcohol or methylated spirit. Storage of animals with limy shells (Crustacea, Mollusca) for a long time in formaline dissolves the shells; they are best preserved in alcohol. Remember that formaline is very poisonous and also injurious to eyes and skin.

Shorts are better than trousers for wading in shallow water. Many animals are most abundant, and some animals like sea-fans are only found at places

4

where they are always submerged in water, even at spring low tides. A cap or hat which can be secured against wind is essential in our climate. Shoes should be with laces; sandals and chappals have a disconcerting habit of ending up with broken straps. It is painful to walk barefooted in mud, for there are always shells with sharp edges, and near cities even broken glass bottles. On rocks overgrown with barnacles thick-soled shoes are a must. Hunter boots are good for shore collection, as long as the treads on the soles are not worn out. Smooth rubber soles involve the risk of slipping and hurting oneself. The black rubberized composition on waterproof shoes meant for wear in the rainy season is ideal as the shoes grip rock firmly. (Gumboots are too heavy.) On very slippery rocks in heavy surf, the three-point contact method of moving is best, i.e. always have either both hands and one foot, or one hand and both feet, in contact with the rocks. On some shores with very flat slopes or high tidal range, the water at high tide can come rushing in faster than you can walk. (You cannot run on uneven, slippery rocks or in soft mud.) Be careful to come out well in time before the incoming tide overtakes you. Or, while collecting on a high patch of ground surrounded by low shore level, you may suddenly find yourself surrounded by water unless you are vigilant. If collecting in the evening, it is a good idea to have an electric torch handy for use, as it may become dark while you are still at some distance from dry, even land.

Many timid animals as well as contractile animals like sea anemones and corals are best seen while submerged. When the sea bottom is exposed, they are either hidden or appear as shapeless blobs. The use of a water-glass from a boat in shallow water enables one to see under water without getting wet. You can make a water-glass by knocking off the bottom from an old bucket and replacing it with a round piece of glass to fit watertight. You hold the bucket so that its bottom is below the water surface and put your head into the bucket. Of course the use of a face mask with snorkel tube is still better, as then you can not only see sea life but also dive down in shallow water to collect it.

THE PROBLEM OF NAMES

Non-biologists are perplexed by the scientific names of plants or animals which, to them, seem unnecessarily complicated or even senseless. So why have scientific nomenclature? There are many reasons for this, the main one being to avoid confusion. Many animals may have the same common or popular name. Thus the cockle of India (*Cardita*) is a different animal from the cockle of Europe or America (*Cardium*). Conversely, one animal may be called by different names in different countries. *Poecilia reticulata*, a very popular fish called a guppy by anyone who keeps pet fish at home, is also known as peacock fish, rainbow fish, millions fish, bellied fish and mosquito fish. If we were to use all these names imagine the confusion of someone not familiar with the fish; he would imagine that we are talking about six different kinds of fish! Add to that the problem of language. A prawn in Gujarat is called 'cholla', in Maharashtra 'kolambi', and in Karnataka 'sunkata'.

Using scientific names avoids all this confusion. The system was established by Linnaeus in the eighteenth century, and is now universally adopted. It is called binomial, because each animal or plant has two names—the generic (equivalent to our surname), written first and always starting with a capital letter, followed by the trivial or specific (equivalent to our personal or 'Christian' name), starting with a small letter. These names are in Latin or latinized versions of other languages. In biological classification, we have two main kingdoms—animal and plant (leaving aside the primitive microscopic forms such as bacteria and viruses). Each kingdom is divided into several phyla (singular phylum), which are further subdivided into classes, orders and families. Interspersed may be subclass, suborder and subfamily. Thus we have the following classification for a common crab:

Kingdom ANIMALIA
Phylum ARTHROPODA
Class CRUSTACEA
Subclass MALACOSTRACA
Order DECAPODA
Suborder BRACHYURA
Family XANTHIDAE
Subfamily OZIINAE
Genus *Ozius*
Species *rugulosus*

So, in spite of Shakespeare's 'What's in a name?', we follow this systematic method of naming in science. It may be noted that the name *Ozius rugulosus* is given to one, and only one, kind of crab. No other animal, let alone crab, will have the same name. At the same time, this crab will have this one name only, and no other name. So any person, anywhere in the world, speaking any language, when he comes across this name, can know precisely which animal is referred to.

Let us now have a look at the different animals found on the seashore. We shall start with the simplest forms—those which evolved earliest—and then go on to the more highly evolved forms.

ANIMALS

PORIFERA

Sponges, although at a casual glance look like plants, are animals, living singly or in colonies of many individuals. (Figure 2.) They have no fixed shape, and form flat encrustations on stones in the region of strong waves. In calmer or deep water, finger-like processes may shoot up, or they may be fan-shaped, branching, tree-like, cup or goblet shaped, trumpet-shaped, or domed forms. Their colours vary as much as the shape, being green, red, yellow, and even black or white. A typical Indian sponge is the bread-crumb sponge (*Tethya*).* Varying in colour from blue, green or pink to yellow ochre, it forms encrustations on stones, from which spring up finger-like lobes. In the crevices of this sponge are found many animals, ranging from tiny crabs and brittle stars to bivalve molluscs.

Another common sponge is the vase-shaped *Tetilla*, resembling a miniature papaya fruit and coloured yellow with a green base. Usually attached loosely to stones, it appears to be quite comfortable even when detached and rolling about in the surf.

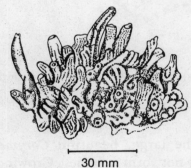

30 mm

Figure 2. Sponges

COELENTERATA

The animals in this phylum have a radial symmetry, and food is captured by means of specialized stinging cells. When a small animal brushes against these, a poisonous fluid is injected into its body, so that it gets paralysed. The stinging cells of some coelenterates are deadly enough to kill fishes and, sometimes, even man. The phylum is divided into three classes.

---

*It may be noted that, in this book, many of the scientific names given will consist of one word only, viz. the genus. This is because, on a vast seashore like India's, a genus may have several species. Identifying all species in a genus will take a lot of space. Moreover, the scope of this book is limited to that of a field-guide; persons who wish to identify species should show their collections to an expert in this line, or take recourse to technical literature.

The Class Hydrozoa consists of branched, feather-like colonies up to 15 cm in extent, and stuck to stones, seaweeds, or even snail-shells. If you look at a colony under a microscope, you will see minute, flower-like shapes, called polypes, on the branches of the colony. These may be naked, or protected inside cup-like hydrotheca. (Figure 3.) A typical example is *Pennaria*, which has white or rosy-pink polypes on an alternately branching yellowish or black stalk. In some colonies of Hydrozoa, the stinging cells are capable, when brushed on the back of the hand, of giving a painful sensation like the bite of a red ant.

|——| 10 mm.

(a) A colony of *Pennaria*

(b) A naked polyp (highly magnified)

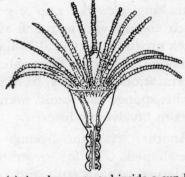

(c) A polyp protected inside a cup-like hydrotheca (highly magnified)

Figure 3.

The large, beautiful *Corymorpha* does not form colonies. Growing to 5 cm high, the mouth is surrounded by two rows of threadlike tentacles, while the slender white stalk ends in a bulbous tip. At the other end is a branched, root-like holdfast, which is buried in mud or sand. (Figure 4.)

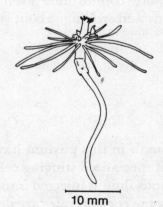

10 mm

Figure 4. *Corymorpha*

The Order Siphonophora, which also belongs to the Hydrozoa, has colonies in which different polypes have different functions (e.g. flotation, defence, digestion, reproduction) and thus have various shapes. They are free-swimming forms with a float at the top. They are described under 'Flotsam and Jetsam' at the end of this book.

The Class Scyphozoa comprises the jellyfishes—translucent, bell-like forms which swim with a pulsating motion. Some are equipped with batteries of deadly stinging cells which can kill a swimmer in minutes. They should, therefore, be handled with care, even when lying apparently dead on the seashore. (Figure 5.)

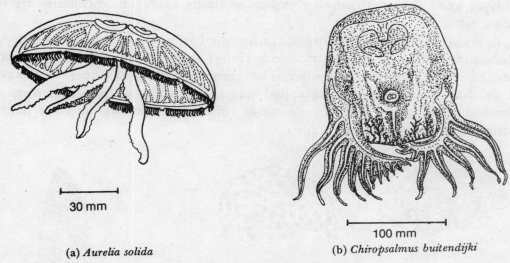

30 mm

(a) *Aurelia solida*

100 mm

(b) *Chiropsalmus buitendijki*

Figure 5. Jellyfishes

In sandy areas we often come across a large pink 'flower'. If we dig it out, we see that it is an orange coloured column-like body with the 'flower' forming its top. The animal is a sea anemone, the petals of the 'flower' being tentacles. (Figure 6.) If you place a small fish on the tentacles, you will see them bending inwards, holding the fish as if with fingers and pushing it into the mouth, which is in the centre of the whorl of tentacles. Undigested food is thrown out of the mouth after some time. When the sea anemone wishes to reproduce, it simply splits into two pieces, each half then growing to form a complete animal. This leads to a mathematical anomaly—the animal uses division to multiply! The sea anemone belongs to the Class Anthozoa.

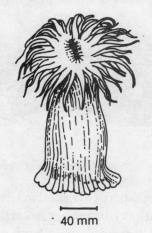

40 mm

Figure 6. Sea Anemone

9

While the sea anemone just described may be as much as 30 cm long, you will find much smaller ones (with the disc only 1 cm in diameter) growing together in large numbers on stones or isolated on boulders. Near a sewage outfall, you may find a veritable carpet of sea anemones growing so close to each other that they look like coral polypes but are soft. Colonies of several polypes grow out of a common expanded fleshy base. These colonies are of *Zoanthus*.

A coral is a colony of tiny sea anemone-like polypes living together in thousands and secreting a calcareous (limy) skeleton of calcium carbonate which they extract out of sea water. They come in myriads of shapes: some have finger-like branches, and are called stag-horn corals, while others form a dome-shaped colony with a network of ridges and furrows, and are hence called brain corals. (Figure 7.)

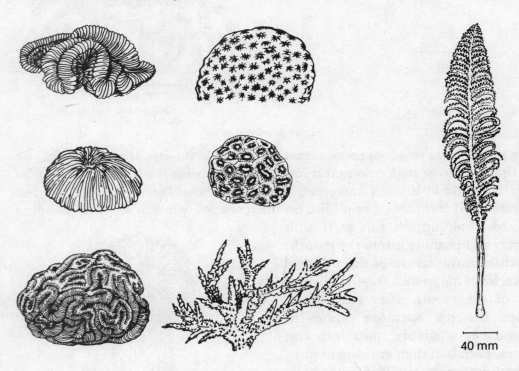

40 mm

Figure 7. Varieties of Coral   Figure 8. Sea-pen (*Virgularia*)

The sea-pen (*Virgularia*) is another colonial form, having a central stalk, with feathery branches on either side on which the polypes are borne. At low tide it is buried, but at high tide it comes above the mud to open its polypes, looking like a feather waving in the current. (Figure 8.)

The sea-pansy or powder-puff (*Cavernularia*) has a short stalk, and the white polypes are borne in a circular arrangement forming a ball. (Figure 9.)

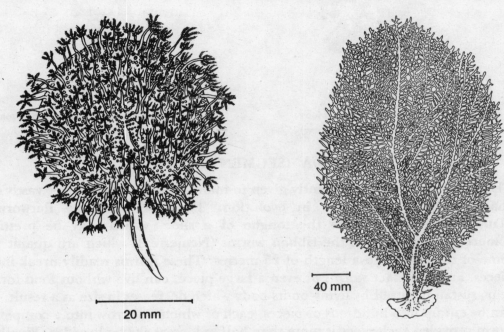

Figure 9. Sea-pansy or Powder-puff (*Cavernularia*)

Figure 10. Sea-fan (*Gorgonium*)

The sea-fan (*Gorgonium*) is yet another colonial form, but it branches only in one plane and the branches may fuse with each other to form the 'fan'. (Figure 10.) White or cream-coloured polypes may grow on a base of contrasting maroon colour, attached to stones by a broad disc-like holdfast. Tiny brittle stars of the same colour and the cowrie-like snail, *Ovulum,* live on sea-fans.

BRYOZOA (OR POLYZOA)

Often you will come across encrustations on stones, seaweeds or shells comprising colonies of tiny animals, which are different in form from the hydroids. Usually they form patches of hard crust of white or yellowish colour. Under a low-power microscope you will be able to see their beatiful sculpture. (Figure 11.) They are colonies of animals popularly called moss-animals. Since identification of these animals is a highly complex task, we shall not treat it here. Suffice it to say that there are something like 3000 species in the world. Examples are *Barentsia* and *Pedicellina*, *Acanthodesia* and *Amathia*. (Figure 12.)

Figure 11. A moss-animal colony
(inset: magnified view)

Figure 12. *Amathia convoluta* — a bryozoan
(magnified)

ANNELIDA (SEGMENTED WORMS)

The name 'worm' is conveniently given to many animals which differ vastly in character and their place in evolution. Thus we have the flatworms (Turbellaria), shaped like the tongue of a shoe, which may be prettily coloured. We also have the ribbon worms (Nemertea), which are quaint as some of them grow to a length of 25 metres. These worms readily break into pieces, and an intact worm, or even a large piece, can live without food for a year, sustaining itself by living on its body which decreases in size as a result. It can be cut up into hundreds of pieces, each of which will grow into a complete worm provided each piece is more than half as long as the body width. Finally, we have the true or segmented worms, belonging to the Phylum Annelida. They may be of diverse shapes, but all, like the earthworm, have a body divided into numerous segments.

Polychaete or segmented worms may be divided into two categories: those that move by swimming or crawling (Errantia), and those that live in a tube built by them (Sedentaria). A typical form such as *Marphysa* has a distinct head with four eyes and armed with jaws that can give a painful nip. (Figure 13.) On each body segment on either side there is a swimming paddle (called parapodium) which is furnished with bristles (setae). This worm can grow to over 30 cm and has a fleshy red colour.

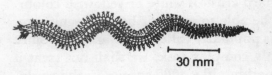

Figure 13. Bristle worm (*Marphysa*)

Figure 14. Scale worm

12

In the scale worms (e.g. *Harmothoe*) the body is covered with a dozen or more pairs of flat scales. (Figure 14.) They are small worms, about 5 cm long, and are usually dark blackish brown in colour.

A worm rather unpleasant to handle is *Eurythoe*. It is a flabby, pink form with brushes of long, colourless, transparent bristles along the parapodia. These bristles readily come off and penetrate the skin like sharp glass splinters, causing great pain.

On beaches formed of a mixture of sand and mud you will often see tubes of mud reinforced with bits of broken shells, coconut husks and seaweeds. About 8 cm of the tough, parchment-like tube extends above the sea bottom, and hundreds of such tubes form a bunch which may be up to a metre long but only 10 – 15 cm wide. These bunches are always parallel to each other and also parallel to the seashore. The buried part of the tube which may be 80 cm long is smooth and parchment-like. The worms (*Diopatra*) living in these tubes are of a pretty iridescent scarlet colour with pulsating, tree-like plumed red gills.

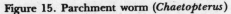

30 mm

40 mm

Figure 15. Parchment worm (*Chaetopterus*)

Figure 16. Lugworm (*Arenicola*)

A rather rare worm is the parchment worm (*Chaetopterus*), which is about 15 cm long and lives in a U-shaped burrow lined with a tube. (Figure 15.) The body is very soft and, when handled, it breaks into two pieces just behind the head. It secretes a copious amount of slime which shines in the dark.

In the terebellid worms (e.g. *Loimia*, *Amphitrite*) which also build tubes of mud, sand and shell fragments, the head has numerous hair-like tentacles in two symmetrical bundles. The worm is 10 – 15 cm long, of a fleshy colour with vivid red gills. (Plate I.) The tentacles are always in motion, stretching out and contracting, bringing sand grains in to build or repair its tube. If the tentacles

13

get broken and detached, they will wriggle about and squirm like living worms for hours.

The lugworm (*Arenicola*) is not very common in India. (Figure 16.) It, too, lives in a U-shaped burrow, but prefers filthy surroundings. It is about 20 cm long and dirty green with brownish red, tufted gills. The worm has a peculiar feeding habit: it simply swallows the mud in which it lives and extracts therefrom the contained organic matter. Its presence can be known from the small piles of mud cast out from its gut outside its burrow.

Of the sedentary, tube-dwelling worms, there are two main groups. In sabellid worms (e.g. *Pectinaria*) the tubes are made of mud or fine sand and are parchment-like in texture, while in serpulid worms (e.g. *Potamoceros*) the tube is hard, coiled or unevenly twisted and calcareous (limy). Tube-dwelling worms are called fan worms, peacock worms or Christmas tree worms. A series of eyes are borne on the 'fan', so that even a shadow is sufficient to make them retreat into their tubes. (Plate I.)

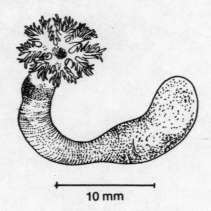

10 mm

Figure 17. Peanut worm (*Dendrostoma*)

Lastly we come to a tiny 'worm' whose position in evolution is disputed. Put in the group Gephyrea, it is a sipunculid known as the peanut worm (*Dendrostoma*), is ivory white in colour, 3 – 4 cm long, and is found in the fissures of rocks. (Figure 17.) The pear-shaped body resembles that of a sea-cucumber, having a retractile proboscis with six tree-like clusters of tentacles.

ARTHROPODA (Class CRUSTACEA)

Phylum Arthropoda is one of the most extensive on earth, including as it does the insects on land. Animals belonging to this phylum have a segmented body but, unlike the numerous segments in worms, they are limited in number. The legs (appendages) are jointed. The body is encased in an armour of chitin (a substance similar to horn) which may be further thickened with lime.

Except for a few sea spiders (Arachnoidea), all the arthropods living in the sea belong to the Class Crustacea, animals breathing by means of gills.

In the salt pans will be found the brine shrimp (*Artemia salina*), related to the fairy shrimps. (Figure 18.) They are tiny (1 − 1.5 cm long), cherry-red creatures swimming on their backs with the help of many pairs of swimming paddles. Brine shrimps are peculiar in many ways. Most of the time the population consists only of females, which do not require the help of males to breed. Moreover, the eggs can be dried and kept alive for years; when put into dilute sea-water, the young are born in a day or two.

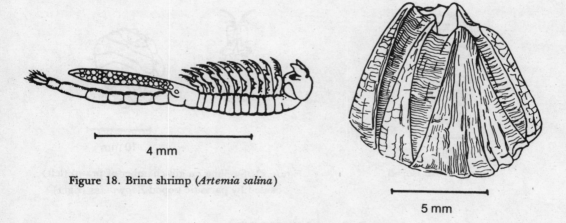

Figure 18. Brine shrimp (*Artemia salina*)

5 mm

Figure 19. Acorn barnacle (*Balanus*)

Acorn barnacles (*Balanus*) may be easily mistaken by the tyro to be molluscs (snails). (Figure 19.) They are sessile (fixed, immobile) animals, to be found in the hundreds on stones or concrete structures. When exposed at low tide, they look like white tents or miniature volcanoes. When submerged in water, they open and their curled, feathery legs protrude. These feathery plumes move rhythmically in and out of the 'shell' and form a net which captures small organisms as food. The barnacle has been jocularly compared to a boy standing on his head inside a limestone house and kicking his food into his mouth with his feet! Some barnacles may be 6 cm across, but most grow only to half a centimetre.

The goose barnacle (*Lepas*) is found, attached by a fleshy stalk, to drifting wood, etc. (See 'Flotsam and Jetsam'.)

15

Order ISOPODA

The word Isopoda means 'similar legs'. Here the body is divided, as in insects, into three parts—head, thorax (chest) and abdomen. The head bears two pairs of sessile eyes (i.e. they are not at the end of stalks). The body in all isopods is dorso-ventrally depressed (flattened from above downwards) and usually spindle-shaped. (Figure 20.)

Isopods may be free-living or parasitic, sucking the blood of fishes or prawns. Free-living isopods (e.g. *Cirolana*) can be dug out in coarse sand. The gill-chamber of the prawn in which parasitic isopods (e.g. *Bopyroides*) live, develops a distinct swelling which easily indicates that there is a parasite inside. (Figure 21.)

10 mm

Figure 20. An Isopod

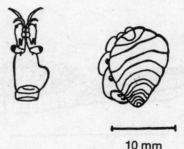

10 mm

Figure 21. Swelling on gill-chamber of prawn (left) caused by parasitic isopod *Bopyroides* (right)

Order AMPHIPODA

These animals are basically similar to Isopods, but a difference immediately noticeable is that they are laterally compressed (i.e. flattened from side to side). (Figure 22.) The result is that when they are held on a flat surface such as the palm of the hand, they cannot stand upright but fall on one side. They are, therefore, called side-swimmers.

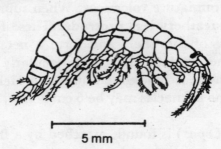

5 mm

Figure 22. Side-swimmer

16

Members of the family Caprellidae have highly elongated forms which resemble the walking-stick insects. The skeleton shrimps (*Caprella*) are so perfectly camouflaged that they cannot be easily detected even when occurring in large numbers on a hydroid colony. (Figure 23.) The usual method of collecting them is to bring such a colony home and keep it in sea-water in a jar overnight. By the next day most of the skeleton shrimps will have left the hydroid colony and sunk to the bottom. It is amusing to watch their antics with a magnifying glass. They seem to bow slowly and with ceremonial grace, like the Japanese; at another moment they clasp their palm-like claws to strike an attitude of prayer!

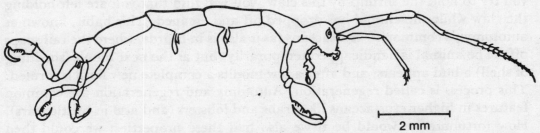

2 mm

Figure 23. Skeleton shrimp (*Caprella*)

Order DECAPODA

Probably the largest and most varied Order among marine Crustacea is Decapoda, comprising highly evolved forms with ten walking legs. The first pair of legs are usually modified as claws. The eggs are carried attached to swimming paddles below the abdomen. The eyes are borne on the tips of stalks.

Prawns (*Peneus*) are such a common sight in fish markets that there is no need to describe them in detail. The first three pairs of legs end in minute claws. The prawn has a serrated (saw-toothed) snout. (Figure 24.) Peneid

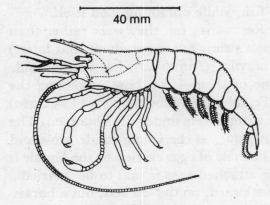

40 mm

Figure 24. Prawn

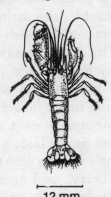

12 mm

Figure 25. Pistol Shrimp (*Alpheus*)

17

prawns do not carry eggs attached to their swimmerets but drop them into the sea.

In cariid prawns the third pair of legs does not have claws, and they carry their eggs attached to the swimmerets. Most interesting among the cariid prawns are the pistol or snapper shrimps (*Alpheus*). (Figure 25.) This animal is more often heard than seen. If you stand at the edge of a rock pool you will hear the metallic clicks of pistol shrimps all around you. When such a shrimp is caught and kept in a glass jar, the click resonates so much that it sounds as if the glass jar has cracked. It is made by the shrimp suddenly snapping its 'thumb' (last joint) of the larger claw against its 'palm' (second-last joint). If you try to hold the shrimp by this claw, you will find that you are left holding the claw while the animal has dropped off and escaped. This habit, known as autotomy, is common in crustaceans (as it also is in lizards, where the tail snaps off). The animal is handicapped temporarily, but at the next moult (shedding of shell) a bud appears, and after a few moults a complete new limb is formed. This process is called regeneration. Autotomy and regeneration are common features in higher crustaceans like crabs and lobsters (and also in brittle stars). How fortunate we would be if we also had these properties; we could then discard a broken arm or leg and grow a new one! Pistol shrimps are usually found in pairs (a male and a female).

Another queer creature is the cleaner shrimp (*Stenopus*). A pair of cleaner shrimps set up a 'station' on a rock or coral head and stand on it, waving their claws upward. Fishes which have wounds or parasites on them seem to know where the shrimps are available; they swim there and indicate their need to be 'serviced' by adopting a head-down posture or by changing their body colour. The shrimp then climbs on to the fish's body and removes the parasites and injured tissue. It even crawls into the fish's gill-chamber, but the fish makes no attempt to swallow it, holding its breath while the shrimp is inside. This partnership enables the shrimp to help the fish, while obtaining food itself.

Lobsters and crayfish belong to the Reptantia, i.e. they walk rather than swim. (This is not to say that they cannot swim, but more about that later.) The spiny lobster, also called marine crayfish (*Panulirus*), has innumerable spines of various sizes on its body, some of them—like those protecting the eyes—being much longer. (Figure 26.) Female spiny lobsters (as well as crabs) carry thousands of eggs attached to the swimmerets under the abdomen. The eggs, when newly laid, are orange-yellow, but, as the young inside grow and absorb the yolk, the eggs turn greyish. The mass of eggs carried by the female is called a 'berry', and an animal carrying attached eggs is said to be 'berried'.

Lobsters normally walk, forward or backward, on the sea bed, but a harassed lobster will dart backward through the water by rapid flips of its powerful

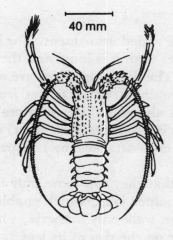

Figure 26. Spiny lobster (*Panulirus*)   Figure 27. Mole crab (*Emerita asiatica*)

abdomen. It can thus swim for a few metres.

Linking lobsters and crabs in evolution are the hermit crabs (*Pagurus*). (Plate I.) In this animal, while the front part of the body is encased in a hard shell, the abdomen is soft. To protect it, the hermit crab seeks an empty snail shell of the correct size and thrusts its abdomen into it. It carries the shell along. Since the abdomen has to be accomodated in a spirally coiled shell, it is asymmetric, being bent to one side.

Another fascinating example of partnership is found in hermit crabs. Many hermit crabs have one or more small sea anemones attached to their shell. The sea anemones protect the hermit crab from enemies, while they get a free ride and bits of food when the hermit crab feeds.

The mole crab (*Emerita*) has an egg-shaped body about 5 cm long, with eyes at the end of thin, long stalks which look like matchsticks. (Figure 27.) It is found in large colonies buried in sand with only its eyes and feelers above the surface. As the tide comes in and covers the burrows, these crabs move upwards along the beach, again digging themselves in quickly.

The porcelain crab (*Petrolisthes*) has a crab-like shape, as its abdomen is loosely tucked below the rather soft body. (Plate I.) Its claws are large, with flattened fingers. The last pair of legs is much reduced and is positioned along the sides of the body. The claws and legs are very readily shed when the crab is handled. Porcelain crabs are abundant; practically every time you overturn a stone you will see them scuttling away into hiding. Some species are beautifully coloured scarlet with sinuous white lines. Some live as commensals with worms or molluscs.

CRABS

True crabs (suborder Brachyura) are a vast and varied assortment. The body, except in some primitive spider crabs, is broader than it is long, and the flap-like abdomen is folded tightly under the body. The first pair of legs are always modified as claws. Eggs are carried by the female, attached to her feathery swimmerets. Sometimes, between the body and abdominal flap of a crab you may see a shapeless yellowish brown mass. This is a parasite (*Sacculina*) which is, surprisingly, related to barnacles. A male crab attacked by this parasite becomes a female.

The legs of crabs are jointed in such a way that they can move only in one plane, like our elbow joint (and unlike our shoulder joint, which enables the arm to move in any direction). Thus a crab can walk only sideways, which it does, when under water, in an elegant manner on the tips of its legs.

The commoner varieties of crabs are shown in Plate II.

One of the most primitive crabs is *Dromia*, with a ball-like, hairy body and brightly coloured forelegs ending in claws. (Figure 28.) If you look carefully at the last two pairs of legs, you will find that they are much smaller than the other legs. Their last joint ends in a hooked tip. These legs are used to hold a piece of sponge over the crab's back. The crab breaks off a piece of live sponge, carefully trims this to fit closely over its back and carries it about. The sponge camouflages the crabs, so that to a casual observer it looks like a walking sponge.

Figure 28. Sponge-crab (*Dromia*)
(hair removed from left half)

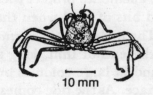

Figure 29. Masked crab (*Dorippe*)

The masked crab (*Dorippe*), a small, flat, drab-looking crab also has its last two pairs of legs similarly hooked. (Figure 29.) However, rather than sponge, it carries one valve (shell) of a bivalve mollusc, and if it cannot get hold of a suitable one, it will even carry a dried leaf over its back.

The box crab (*Calappa*) has a globular body coloured to resemble sand, but with bright maroon speckles, streaks and spots near the rear border. If you turn it over, you will find that the sides of the carapace are expanded into thin, plate-like hollows under which the legs can be partially withdrawn. The claws are flat and shaped like shovels, with large, saw-toothed upper edges. The crab usually buries itself in sand until only its eyes are visible, holding its claws tightly against the front part of its body so as to prevent sand grains and other matter from being sucked into its breathing holes.

A related crab is *Matuta*, a pretty sulphur-yellow crab with a rhomboid carapace with two long spines extending along its sides. A series of violet spots or irregular loops (which turn red when the crab is preserved) stipple the body. However, the most obvious difference is that while the legs we have seen in the crabs described so far end in sharp tips, in *Matuta* they are elegantly flattened to form swimming paddles. The crab can swim daintily but is handicapped on dry land as it cannot walk. You can sometimes see the crab stranded on a mud flat or beach.

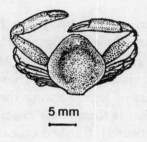

5 mm

Figure 30. Porcelain crab (*Philyra*)

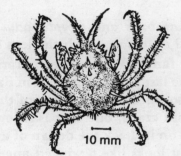

10 mm

Figure 31. Thornback crab (*Paramithrax*)

The porcelain crabs (*Philyra*) have small (1 cm wide) globular, pebble-shaped bodies coloured brown above and white below. (Figure 30.) Their name is very appropriate as they appear to be made out of baked clay or porcelain. It should be noted that these porcelain crabs are only distantly related to the porcelain crabs belonging to the *Pestrolisthes* group (which are not true crabs.)

The spider crabs are a heterogeneous group, with rather long legs, and usually with a vase or pitcher-shaped body with sharp spines scattered over it, meant for protection against enemies. The thornback crab (*Paramithrax*) (Figure 31) breaks off pieces of seaweed and plants them on its back, where they are fixed with the help of the spines and tiny hooks. A crab fully 'dressed' in this manner looks like a veritable walking garden!

Most spidery of all the spider crabs is *Doclea*, which has a globular hairy body, and with legs 3¾ times as long as the body, looking like a marine daddy-long-legs. (Figure 32.)

21

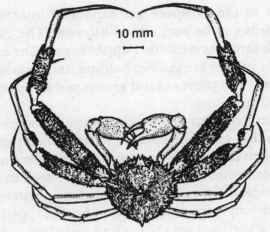

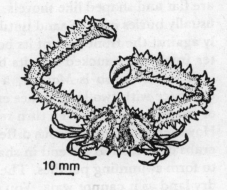

Figure 32. Spider crab (*Doclea*)

Figure 33. *Lambrus*

In *Lambrus* and *Cryptopodia* the under-surface of the body has hollow, vaulted spaces in which the legs can be folded, out of view. (Figure 33.)

The family Portunidae comprises swimming crabs, but, unlike in *Matuta*, only the last pair of legs ends in flattened swimming paddles, so that these crabs can also walk with the help of the three other pairs of legs. Among the many Portunid crabs, one that is sure to attract attention is *Charybdis cruciata*. It carries on its back the design of a perfect cross (or sword), flanked on each side by what looks like a winged angel!

Then we have many kinds of walking crabs (family Xanthidae), but we need not describe all of them. One, the hirsute crab (*Pilumnus*), deserves mention, as not only its body, but even the legs and claws (except the fingers) are clothed in a shaggy coat of stiff hairs. (Figure 34.)

Unlike most crabs which can fend for themselves, the pea crab (*Pinnotheres*), or at least its female, lives inside the shells of a live bivalve mollusc, where it feeds on the minute food particles gathered on its host's gills. (Figure 35.)

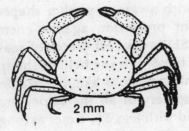

Figure 34. Hirsute crab (*Pilumnus*)

Figure 35. Pea crab (*Pinnotheres*)

22

Among the crabs which are slowly evolving from marine to terrestrial forms are those of the family Ocypodidae. Ghost crabs (*Ocypode*) are found on the higher reaches of sandy beaches. (Figure 36.) Coloured like sand, they scamper so fast on the beach that it is almost impossible to catch them in daytime. At night they can be hyptonized by shining an electric torch into their eyes. Incidentally, the eyes in adults, unlike in other crabs, are not situated at the tips of the eyestalks, but along one side near the tip, looking like partially nibbled ice candy! While running about when chased, these crabs may suddenly stop, when their body colour so matches the sand that they seem to disappear into thin air—hence their popular name. They can live for weeks outside water as long as their gill-chambers hold a little water.

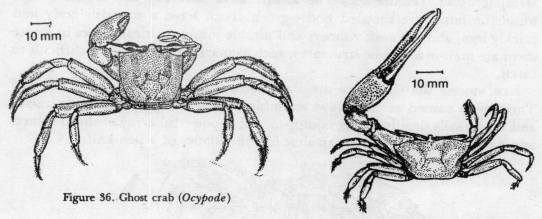

Figure 36. Ghost crab (*Ocypode*)

Figure 37. Fiddler or dhobi crab
(*Uca* or *Gelasimus*)

Allied to the ghost crabs are the fiddler or dhobi crabs (*Uca* or *Gelasimus*). (Figure 37.) On sandy flats interspersed with a little mud, at ebb tide they can be seen in large numbers, the males waving their enormously huge claws about to beckon females. Only one of the claws in the male is developed to this huge size—larger and heavier than the body; the other claw is tiny, as are both the claws in the female. The waving action of the male claw is likened to the scraping of a bow on a fiddle or the action of a dhobi (washerman) striking clothes on a rock to clean them—hence the popular name.

Allied to the fiddler crabs are the soldier crabs (*Dotilla*). (Figure 38.) In case one wonders what is so martial about them (since they look, and in fact are, weaklings), it is their occurrence in enormous numbers on a patch of sand. They can be detected by the star-like radiating pattern of lines of tiny balls made of sand, in the centre of which is the burrow. The burrows literally riddle the ground.

23

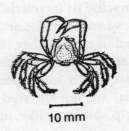

Figure 38. Soldier crab (*Dotilla*)

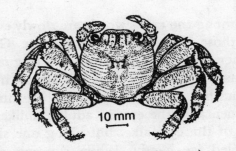

Figure 39. Rock crab (*Grapsus*)

Finally, we come to the rock crabs (family Grapsidae), such as *Grapsus* and *Metopograpsus*. (Figure 39.) The former have dark red and cream bands, while the latter are mottled bottle-green. Both have a squarish body and prickly legs, and are swift runners and nimble jumpers. Ideal places to locate them are man-made stone structures, such as marinas, but they are difficult to catch.

Last among the Crustacea are the mantis shrimps (*Squilla*). (Figure 40.) They are so named as their claws resemble those of the praying mantis insect, and are equally deadly, being equipped with a powerful array of sharp spines, and having the capacity to snap shut like the blades of a pen-knife.

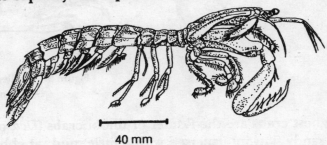

Figure 40. Mantis shrimp (*Squilla*)

The spiders have a few marine relatives. The horseshoe crab (*Tachypleus gigas*), also known as king crab, has a flat, horseshoe-shaped body completely covering the legs. (Figure 41.) Behind the abdomen is the long spike-like tail. In India it occurs only on the shores of the Bay of Bengal, growing to 60 cm.

The sea spiders, also called no-body crabs, have four pairs of very long, slender walking legs with a smaller fifth pair. (Figure 42.) The body consists of a small cephalothorax with a minute, rudimentary abdomen. As in the sea horse, the male carries the eggs after they have been laid by the female. Sea spiders occur in shallow waters among seaweeds and hydroids, where they are very difficult to detect.

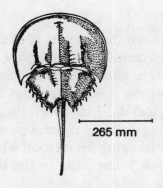

Figure 41. Horseshoe crab
(*Tachypleus gigas*)

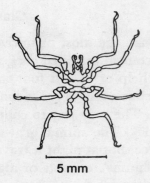

Figure 42. Sea spider or no-body crab
(*Anoplodactylus*)

MOLLUSCA

This phylum comprises what are popularly called sea-shells, because the novice usually comes across shells on the beach and may not realize that they once contained living animals. Sea-shells are divided into two main classes—snails (Gastropoda) which have spirally twisted shells, and bivalves (Pelecypoda) which live between two plain (i.e. not spiral) valves of shell. There are also the coat-of-mail shells belonging to the Amphineura and the elephant's tusk shells (Scaphopoda) whose shells differ radically in shape both from the snails and the bivalves.

The coat-of-mail shell (*Chiton*) has a symmetrical body covered on top by a 'shell' made up of eight separate plates. (Figure 43.) It grows to 3 − 4 cm long and is found adhering to stones.

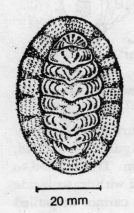

Figure 43. Coat-of-mail shell
(*Chiton*)

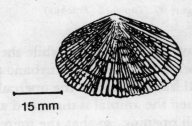

Figure 44. Limpet
(*Cellana*)

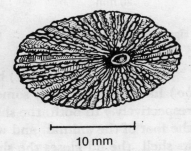

Figure 45. Keyhole limpet
(*Diodora*)

25

Class GASTROPODA

In this Class, the most primitively evolved animals are the limpets (*Cellana*), having a conical uncoiled shell under which the soft animal lives. (Figure 44.) With the help of its soft foot the animal can create a partial vacuum, and it sticks so tenaciously to rocks that it is impossible to prise it off once it has been disturbed. The only way to collect it is to slip a scalpel deftly between the foot and the rock. The animal grows to 2 or 3 cm. During daytime it remains stuck at one place, but at night it travels a metre or more foraging for its food which, like the Chitons', consists of algae. It always returns 'home', i.e. to the same place on the rock from where it started.

Allied to the limpets are the keyhole limpets (*Diodora*). (Figure 45.) In these, the shell has a small hole at the top in the centre, from which faecal matter (undigested food) is thrown out along with excess water.

The ear-shell (*Haliotis*) is again an apt name. (Figure 46.) The shell is shaped like the human ear and has a row of holes along one margin. The outer surface of the shell is limy white, but the inside has a beautiful pearly iridescence, caused by a layer of mother-of-pearl secreted by the animal. While Indian ear-shells grow up to 4 cm in length, the related abalones of North America grow to a gigantic 25 – 30 cm.

 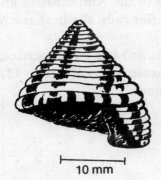 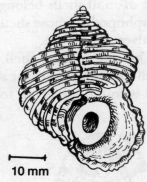

20 mm   10 mm   10 mm

Figure 46. Ear-shell (*Haliotis*)   Figure 47. Top-shell (*Trochus*)   Figure 48. Turban-shell
(*Turbo intercostalis*)

The top-shells (*Trochus*) have a conical shell, while the turban-shells (*Turbo*) have a coiled shell somewhat resembling a turban. (Figures 47 and 48, respectively.) In both, the shell has a lid called the operculum. This is fixed to the foot of the animal, and when the animal is disturbed and withdraws inside its shell, the lid closes the shell opening, so that the animal cannot be pulled out. The operculum in *Turbo* is plano-convex (rounded on one side and flat on the other) and is called cat's eye. Although the outer surface of the shell is drab, if this is removed by dissolving in dilute acid, an exquisite layer of mother-of-pearl is exposed. Large *Trochus* and *Turbo* (found in the Andaman and Nicobar Islands) are thus prepared and made into knick-knacks like ash trays, *agarbatti* stands, flower vases, etc.

A related snail is the button-shell (*Umbonium*). (Plate I.) Growing to the size of a shirt button, it is one of the daintiest sea-shells, showing a variety of colours and designs, ranging from ivory white to pink to gray blue to chestnut brown. They are found in thousands on beaches.

Nerita, found on rocky shores, is heavy for its size (2 cm). (Figure 49.) Its shell is extraordinarily thick, probably to allow it to be tumbled about in the strong surf.

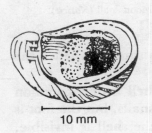

Figure 49. Nerite (*Nerita*)

Figure 50. Periwinkle
(*Littorina undulata*)

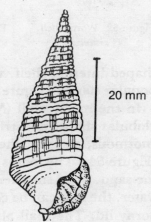

Figure 51. Horn-shell
(*Potamides palustris*)

The periwinkle (*Littorina*) is found on rocky shores or marinas. (Figure 50.) Although small in size, it occurs in large numbers and is most abundant on the highest reaches of spring tides—sometimes where it is never submerged even at high tide but only sprayed by the surf (splash zone).

The horn-shells (*Potamides*) have elongated shells with the spiral whorls ornamented with ridges and tubercles. (Figure 51.) They are scavengers, found in large numbers on mud flats.

The worm-shells (*Vermetus*) can be mistaken by the novice for serpulid worms. (Figure 52.) The shell starts off as a tight spiral, but as it grows it starts uncoiling and ends up as a twisted tube, as if the animal had forgotten how to build the typical spirally coiled shell! The shell is cemented to rocks or corals just as are worm tubes.

In the cup-and-saucer limpet (*Calyptraea*), the shell is not spirally coiled and thus resembles a limpet, but the original shell spire is represented by a cup-

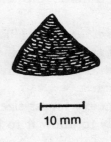

Figure 52. Worm-shell
(*Vermetus*)

Figure 53. Cup-and-saucer
limpet (*Calyptraea*)

Figure 54. Moon snail (*Natica*)

shaped internal shelf, with the shell surrounding it like a saucer, whence the popular name. (Figure 53.)

In the moon snail (*Natica*), a carnivorous snail, the shell is of a common globular shape, not strikingly different from many other snails, but the foot is enormous, so that when this is fully extended most of the shell is invisible. (Figure 54.) The foot is used to burrow rapidly and glide like a plough through the sand, or to smother its prey by covering it. By ejecting a large amount of water, the foot can be completely withdrawn into the shell, which is closed by a horny lid. The snail also has a file-like tongue which can bore a hole into a clam or mussel shell and pick out its flesh for food.

Natica is also called the sand-collar snail. The egg-case of the snail, containing well nigh half a million tiny eggs, looks like a collar. It also resembles the rubber plunger used by plumbers to open clogged drains. (Figure 55.)

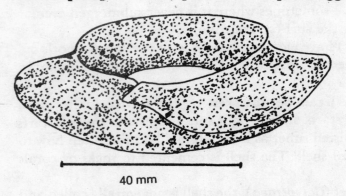

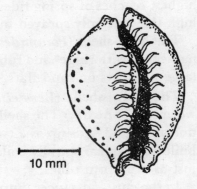

Figure 55. Egg capsule of *Natica*

Figure 56. Cowrie (*Cypraea*)

Cowries (*Cypraea*) are some of the most popularly known snails. (Figure 56 and Plate III.) The adult shell, on the outside, gives no indication of a spiral structure, having a narrow slit-like opening from which the foot and mantle lobes may protrude. The mantle lobes are wide flaps which come up over the sides of the polished shell so that, in life, only the top centre of the shell remains uncovered.

Related forms like *Ovulum* are found on sea-tans (*Gorgonium*), the snail exactly matching the colour of its host. (Figure 57).

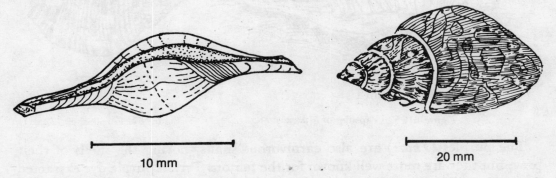

10 mm

20 mm

Figure 57. Flamingo's tongue shell (*Ovulum*)   Figure 58. Whelk (*Babylonia spirata*)

Whelks are fairly large and heavily built scavengers. *Babylonia spirata* has a white shell blotched with red; in the living animal this is covered by a brown horny outer skin. (Figure 58.) The dog-whelk (*Nassa, Nassarius*) is a smaller snail with a long, conspicuous siphon. It can be seen in large numbers around a dead fish or crab on the shore.

The murices (*Murex*) have stout shells which vary in shape in the different species. (Figures 59 and 60.) They are carnivorous snails like *Natica*, but while

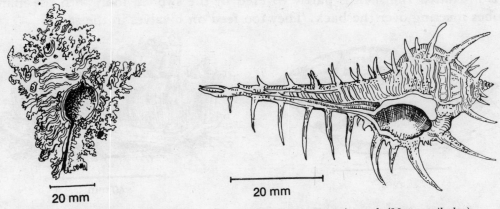

20 mm

20 mm

Figure 59. Murice (*Murex adustus*)   Figure 60. Venus's comb (*Murex tribulus*)

29

the latter attack buried prey, murices drill holes in bivalves living on the sea bed. Some species (e.g. *Murex tribulus*, *Murex tenuispina*) have spines on the shell. Their eggs are laid in tubular egg cases. (Figure 61.)

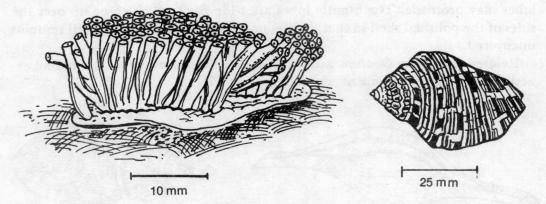

Figure 61. Egg capsules of *Murex*   Figure 62. Purple shell (*Thais*)

The purples (*Thais*) are also carnivorous snails, boring the shells of their prey, but they are more well known for the famous Tyrian purple dye extracted from them. (Figure 62.) The eggs are laid in vase-shaped, flattened capsules. The adults eat snail eggs, including their own. In each egg-case there are many eggs with not enough yolk to nourish all the young, with the result that the young start eating each other inside the egg-case until only one emerges from the case. If the snail is crushed a milky white fluid oozes out which, on exposure to sunlight, changes gradually to yellow, green, blue, crimson and finally to purple.

The olives (*Oliva*) have beautifully polished, elongated shells, each with a short, pyramidal spire and a very long narrow opening (mouth). (Figure 63.) As in *Natica* the shell is partly covered by the swollen foot, with the mantle lobes meeting over the back. They too feed on bivalves in the sand.

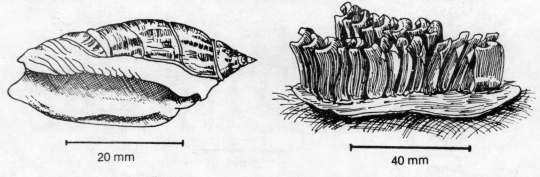

Figure 63. Olive shell (*Oliva*)   Figure 64. Egg capsules of Cone shell (*Conus*)

The cones (*Conus*) resemble olives in the shape of their shell, but the spire is still shorter and compressed. (Plate III.) Shells of the many species of this genus are collectors' items, but one should be careful about handling them. The tongue of this snail is modified into tiny darts which are ejected by the snail with force and can penetrate the fingers. Their barbed tips contain venom which causes intense pain and, in some cases, even death in man. The eggs are laid in vase-shaped, flattened capsules. (Figure 64.)

Highly modified 'snails' are the sea hares (*Aplysia, Notarchus*). (Figure 65.) They can be seen in large numbers among seaweeds in winter, their bottle-green colour merging with the green of the seaweed *Ulva*. They may grow to 30 cm length, but are soft and flabby. The body is contained within the hump-like 'back', with a stumpy head with two pairs of tentacles in front, and a broad foot passing into a 'tail' behind. The thin, transparent, fragile 'shell' is completely hidden inside the body. The sea hare lays its eggs in long yellow strings which look like an entangled ball of thick twine; each string may contain as many as 86,000,000 eggs. (Figure 66.) When touched or lifted, the adults release a purple fluid which looks like a solution of potassium permanganate but is not harmful to our skin.

Figure 65. Sea hare (*Aplysia*)   Figure 66. Egg ribbon of sea hare

In *Notarchus*, a cousin of *Aplysia*, the body is covered all over with branched hairy protuberances and the green skin has iridescent peacock blue-green spots lined with orange, about 3 − 4 mm in diameter. Sea hares are hermaphrodites, i.e. both the sexes are contained in the same animal. Thus an animal may act either as a male or a female, or simultaneously as both. It is a common sight on the mud flats to see a 'Roman ring' of as many as eight to ten individuals mating, an individual acting as a male for its partner ahead and as a female to its partner behind it.

Finally we come to the sea slugs (nudibranchs). The name does not do justice to these exquisitely pretty creatures; they are so unlike the drab and ugly slugs found in gardens. There are two main groups. The *Doris* group slugs have flat, circular, warty bodies, and breathe by means of a circlet of feathery gills situated near the hind end. (Plate III.) If you pick up a Dorid and place it undisturbed in a bowl of sea-water, after some time you will find the retracted (withdrawn) gills come out like a flower from the vent.

Members of the *Aeolis* group have elongated ploughshare-like bodies, bearing on the upper surface the false gills. These may be clusters of filaments or nipple-like protuberances. (Plate III.)

Nudibranchs are found in the lower inter-tidal region, as they cannot tolerate desiccation. Aeolids are usually found on hydroid colonies; not only can they feed on these venomous creatures, but the stinging cells of the prey remain alive, unaltered and active inside the nudibranch. Thus larger animals will not eat the nudibranchs so protected by stinging cells.

Class PELECYPODA

In this Class the shell consists of two valves, hence the popular name bivalve. The gills, in addition to serving as breathing organs, act as filters to collect microscopic food particles.

Windowpane oysters (*Placuna placenta*) have very flat circular shells, up to 15 cm around, and are found living in mud. (Figure 67.) The thin pearly shell has the appearance of mica and was earlier used for glazing windows by the Chinese and Portuguese; some old mansions in Goa still have such windows.

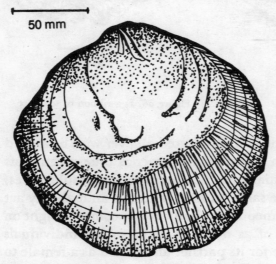

50 mm

Figure 67. Windowpane oyster (*Placuna placenta*) (one valve)

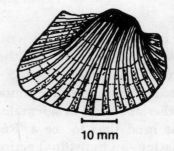

10 mm

Figure 68. One valve of ark shell (*Arca*)

Ark shells (*Arca*), found in mud flats, superficially resemble cockles in their ribbed shells. (Figure 68.) Instead of the colourless molluscan blood, *Arca granosa* and some others have red blood which imparts a red colour to the flesh. For this reason the meat is considered nutritive and is fed to pregnant women.

Green mussels (*Perna*—formerly *Mytilus*—*viridis*) attach themselves to rocks. (Figure 69.) This is done by means of a thread called 'byssus', secreted by the animal in liquid form but which hardens in contact with sea-water. Many such byssus threads anchor the mussel to the substrate. The shell grows to 8 cm or more and is dark green.

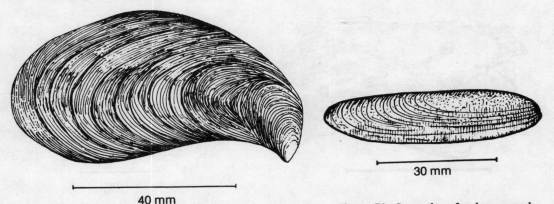

40 mm

Figure 69. Green mussel (*Perna viridis*)
(one valve)

30 mm

Figure 70. One valve of a date mussel
(*Lithophaga*)

The date mussel (*Lithophaga*) is so called because of the shape and dark brown colour of its shell. (Figure 70.) It bores into limestone rocks, corals or large snail shells by secreting an acid. A tough horny covering over its own shell protects it against the acid. This mussel also grows to the same size as the green mussel.

Wing-shells (*Pteria*) are often found on sea-fans. One of the 'ears' (a wing-like projection at the end of the hinge of the shell) is extended to form a spine-like projection. (Figure 71.)

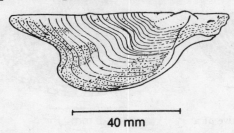

40 mm

Figure 71. One valve of a wing-shell (*Pteria*)

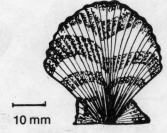

10 mm

Figure 72. One valve of a scallop (*Pecten*)

In the scallop (*Pecten*), too, the hinge has prominent ears, and the shell has ribs. (Figure 72.) Along the fringe of the mantle is a row of eyes at the tips of the marginal tentacles, and when disturbed it can 'swim' crudely by flapping its shell-valves open and shut.

The edible oyster (*Crassostrea*) has one valve permanently cemented to a rock, with the smaller valve hinged to it. (Figure 73.)

Cockles (*Cardita*), with their thick, heart-shaped, ribbed shells, resemble *Arca*. The common form has an ivory-white shell with red spots on the ribs. (Plate I.) With its muscular sickle-shaped foot, it is able to hop along the sea bed.

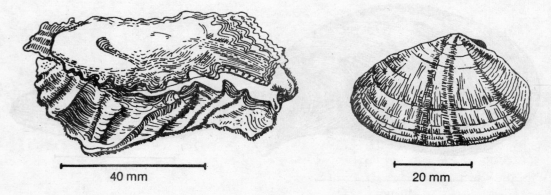

Figure 73. Rock oyster (*Ostrea crenulifera*)   Figure 74. One valve of the wedge shell (*Donax*)

Wedge shells (*Donax*) have their rear end truncate. (Figure 74.) They are purely marine, never entering backwaters, and grow to 4 cm long. The backwater clams (*Meretrix*) are equally plentiful but prefer estuarine conditions and have symmetrical shells. (Figure 75.) Tapestry shells (*Paphia*) are so called from their markings (in some species only); similarly designed is *Sunetta*. (Figures 76 and 77 respectively)

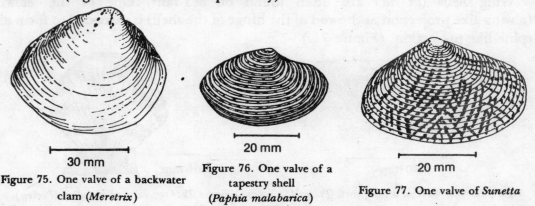

Figure 75. One valve of a backwater clam (*Meretrix*)

Figure 76. One valve of a tapestry shell (*Paphia malabarica*)

Figure 77. One valve of *Sunetta*

The piddock (*Pholas*) is a pretty, white, delicate looking shell, shaped like an angel's wing. (Figure 78.) The suface is covered with rasp-like prickles, and the animal bores into soft clayey rocks by turning the shell to and fro like a carpenter's bradawl.

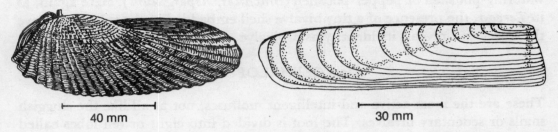

40 mm

30 mm

Figure 78. One valve of piddock or
angel's wing (*Pholas*)

Figure 79. One valve of the razor shell (*Solen*)

The razor shell (*Solen*) has two elongated, rectangular valves resembling an old-fashioned barber's razor. (Figure 79.) The muscular foot enables it to burrow extremely rapidly in sand. It can burrow faster than we can dig it out. The trick is to put a pinch of salt into the animal's burrow, which will send it scuttling to the top.

Shipworms (*Teredo*) are habituated to boring into wood and are a menace to wooden piers and jetties as well as to boats. On the surface of shipworm-ridden wood you will see a tiny hole barely visible to the naked eye. If you split open the wood (which is very easy as the wood becomes brittle) you will see a worm-like shape of the thickness of a pencil. Only a pair of tiny shell-valves at the forward end of the animal reveal its identity as a bivalve mollusc. (Figure 80.) As it bores into the wood, the shipworm coats the tunnel with a liny substance which hardens to form a lining.

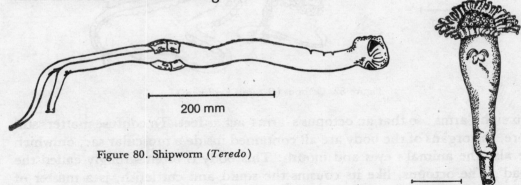

200 mm

Figure 80. Shipworm (*Teredo*)

20 mm

Figure 81. Watering-pot shell or
pepper-pot shell (*Brachites*)

During very low spring tides you may come across, buried upright in the sand, a white cylindrical tube 8 cm long with two or three circlets of frills around the upper end and a closed lower end with many small perforations looking like the 'rose' of a gardener's watering can. (Figure 81.) This is the watering-pot shell or pepper-pot shell (*Brachites, Aspergillum*). Here again, as in *Teredo*, the presence of a tiny bivalve shell embedded in the tube just above the lower end reveals its identity as a bivalve.

Class CEPHALOPODA

These are the most active and intelligent molluscs, not at all like the sluggish snails or sedentary bivalves. The foot is divided into eight or ten lobes called 'arms'. These arms are equipped with a large number of suckers. Each sucker has a round, horny ring, the area inside which can be lifted up by muscles so as to form a partial vacuum. The mouth has a horny beak, remarkably like a parrot's.

Octopi have eight arms, all of equal size. (Figure 82.) Terminology in an octopus is a bit confusing. As stated earlier, the foot of this animal is divided

40 mm

Figure 82. Octopus (*Octopus herdmani*)

into eight 'arms', so that an octopus's 'arms' act as feet. To confuse matters still more, the organs of the body are all contained inside a muscular sac, on which are also the animal's eyes and mouth. This body is often wrongly called the 'head'. The octopus, like its cousins the squid and cuttlefish, is a master of camouflage, and it is fascinating to see even in a freshly dead specimen the rapid expansion and contraction of its pigment cells.

36

Octopi on our coasts do not grow to a large size, the body being the size of a clenched fist, with the arms each about 75 cm long.

Ejecting jets of water from a muscular tube called the siphon, an octopus can swim backwards. When annoyed, it ejects a black 'ink' (called sepia) which discolours the sea-water around it, just like the smoke screen used in military manoeuvres. In the breeding season, the female lays clusters of eggs which hang like grapes from the undersides of rocks, and broods over them.

The cuttlefish (*Sepia*) has a shield-shaped body with a small head at the front end, bearing two eyes and ten arms. (Figure 83 and Plate IV.) Of these, eight are short and stumpy, but two are longer than the body and are called tentacles. In these the suckers on each tentacle are restricted to a fleshy pad at the end. The tentacles are normally retracted into pouches on the head, but can be shot out to capture prey. The body of a cuttlefish is supported by a white, limy 'skeleton' called cuttlebone. This is not visible outside the body, but can be cut out and is then seen to have the same shape as the body, with wavy markings on it; it is light as it contains air spaces. Cuttlefish can also throw a smoke screen around themselves and the black 'ink' was earlier used as sepia dye by artists. Cuttlefish lay clusters of eggs, which are round with a drawn-out tip. (Figure 84.)

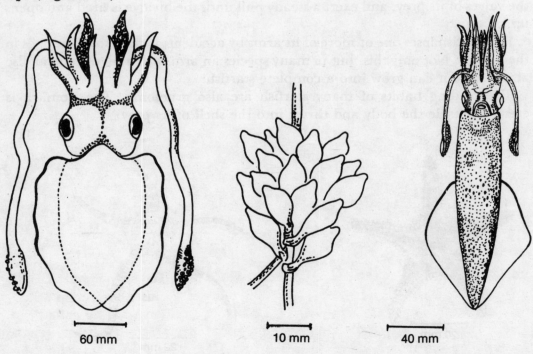

| 60 mm | 10 mm | 40 mm |

Figure 83. Cuttlefish (*Sepia*) Figure 84. Eggs of cuttlefish Figure 85. Squid (*Loligo*)

Squids (*Loligo*) have a torpedo-shaped flesh-coloured body narrower than the cuttlefish, with a wider fringed fin on each side. (Figure 85.) They lack the chalky cuttlebone but, instead, have a transparent horny 'pen'.

ECHINODERMATA

This phylum is characterized by a five-sided symmetry. Numerous small, calcareous plates are embedded in the skin; thus the name of the phylum (*echinos* = hedgehog; *derma* = skin).

Class ASTEROIDEA

This Class comprises the starfishes or sea-stars, typically having five arms around a central disc. (Figure 86.) This number is not, however, fixed, and there may be four or six arms. The arms may be stubby or long in different species. Locomotion is by means of the innumerable tube-feet on the lower surface of the arms. Water can be pumped in and out of these tube-feet, which end in discs similar to the suckers of cephalopods and exert a partial vacuum. The starfish uses the vacuum created by these tube-feet to overcome the muscular resistance of its prey—bivalve molluscs. The starfish's arms wrap over the valves of its prey, and exert a steady pull until the bivalve is tired and opens up.

If a starfish loses one or more of its arms by accident, it can grow new ones in their place. Not only this, but in many species an arm with a bit of central disc attached to it can grow into a complete starfish!

The feeding habits of many starfish are also gruesome. The stomach is everted outside the body and thrust into the shell of its prey.

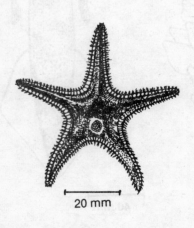

20 mm

Figure 86. Starfish

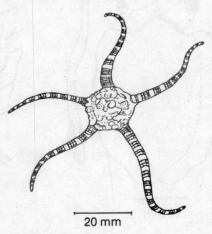

20 mm

Figure 87. Brittle-star

Class OPHIUROIDEA

Brittle-stars resemble starfish in general appearance, but have very slender, many-jointed arms much longer than the tiny central disc. (Figure 87.) The arms are shed at the slightest disturbance, so that it is quite difficult to pick up some species intact. The best way to collect them is to prod them gently so as to make them move over on to a watch-glass held nearby and then lift them up. Many species occur on our shores. *Macrophiothrix* has spiny arms, while *Ophiactis* lives inside sponge crevices and *Ophiothela* lives on sea-fans, having the same colour as the sea-fan.

Class ECHINOIDEA

Sea urchins have a globular body encased in a hard 'test', made up of immovable plates joined together in a regular pattern. Besides the tube-feet, carried in ten rows, there are many spines covering the test; these may be long and needle-like, or short and stubby. (Figure 88.)

In the sand-dollar (also called cake urchin) the body is flattened and disc-like, with a five-rayed petal-like design on the upper side. (Figure 89.)

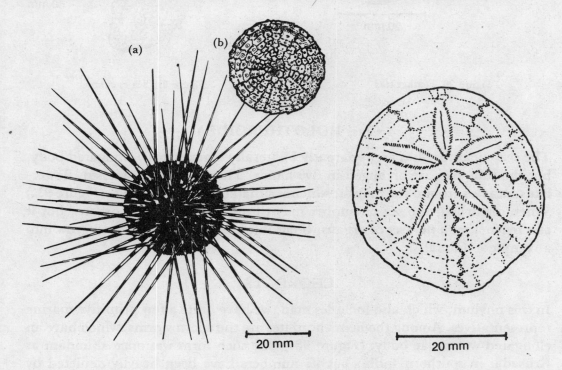

(a) (b)

20 mm

20 mm

Figure 88. (a) Sea urchin (b) 'Test' of sea urchin

Figure 89. Sand dollar

Class CRINOIDEA

Feather stars have usually ten arms bearing close-set branches called pinnules, thus giving the appearance of feathers. (Figure 90.) These spring from shorter appendages called cirri, which are used by the animal to attach itself temporarily. It can swim gracefully by moving the arms up and down.

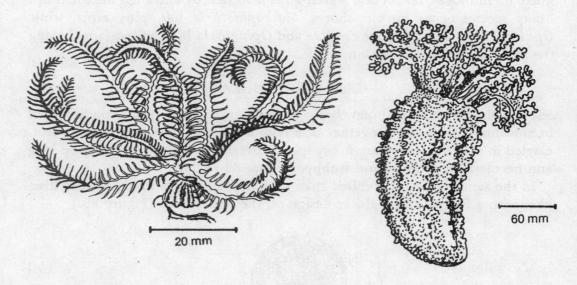

Figure 90. Feather star

20 mm

60 mm

Figure 91. Sea cucumber

Class HOLOTHUROIDEA

The sea cucumber has an apparently bilaterally symmetrical, elongated body, but the tube feet are arranged in five bands. There are ten branched, flower-like tentacles around the mouth, which is situated at the front end. (Figure 91.) When disturbed, the sea cucumber may throw out its internal organs, but it can regenerate a new set of organs. If cut into two, the head-end can grow into a complete animal.

CHORDATA

In this phylum, which also includes man, we have quite a few primitive marine representatives. Among the hemichordates are the acorn worms, which have an elongated worm-like body. (Figure 92.) One such form was once abundant at Krusadai in southern India, but its numbers have been heavily depleted by over-collection.

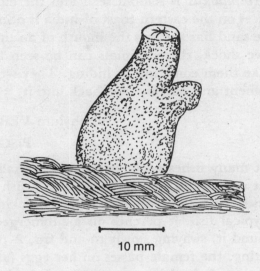

Figure 92. Acorn worm (*Balanoglossus*)

Figure 93. Sea squirt

The subphylum Urochorda is well represented in all seas by the plentiful ascidians or tunicates. Like the Bryozoa, there are many species difficult to identify; the tyro may confuse them with small sponges, but they can be distinguished by their plump, barrel-like bodies with two openings, hence they are also called sea squirts. (Figure 93.) Many species form colonies. Encrusting tunicate colonies may also be distinguished by their smooth, slippery touch, whereas sponges have a gritty texture because of their spicules. Tunicates are brightly coloured—yellow, orange, pink and red being common.

The subphylum Cephalochorda has as its representative *Amphioxus* or lancelets. (Figure 94.) The body, about 5 cm long, is fish-like, laterally compressed and tapered at both ends, with a fin extending along the crest of

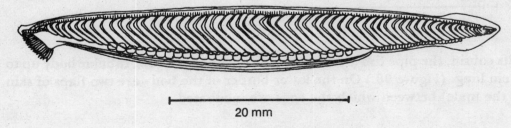

Figure 94. Lancelet (*Amphioxus*)

the animal to expand in the rear into a tail fin. There is no head. On the body surface are many V-shaped muscle segments, with the point of the 'V' directed forward.

Amphioxus is seldom seen and therefore thought to be rare. However, at places on the eastern coast of India it occurs in fair numbers. Wherever a low-tide sand bar shelters the mouth of an unpolluted bay, and is protected from wave shock, these animals can be seen by stamping the ground, which will make them come out of hiding. They writhe about on the sand surface for a moment and quickly dive back into it.

Subphylum VERTEBRATA
PISCES

Not many fishes occur in extremely shallow waters. Prominent among those that do are the ones rarely seen in a fish market. Most well known is the sea horse (*Hippocampus*). (Figure 95.) Looking like the knight in chess rather than a typical fish, it perches on a submerged stick or sea-fan by curling its tail around it, swaying slowly to and fro. A peculiarity in this fish is that, during mating, the female passes on her eggs (and her responsibilities!) to the male. They are lodged in a spongy pouch in the father's body, and on hatching the young escape from a small opening, so that it is the father that appears to 'give birth' to young, and not the mother!

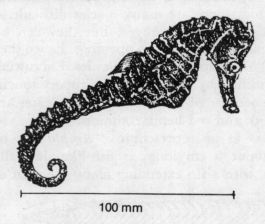

Figure 95. Seahorse (*Hippocampus kuda*)

100 mm

Its cousin, the pipe fish (*Syngnathus*), has a long, narrow, tubular body up to 15 cm long. (Figure 96.) On the lower border of the body are two flaps of skin (in the male) between which the eggs are incubated.

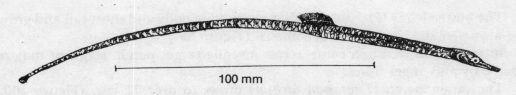

Figure 96. Pipefish (*Syngnathus spicifer*)

Very common on mud flats are the mudskippers or gobies (*Periophthalmus*). (Figure 97.) Basking on the mud, they look very intelligent with their vigilant ever-moving eyes. A slight disturbance and off they go hopping into the water. Their pelvic fins are fused to form a disc-like sucker which enables them to stick on an inclined stone.

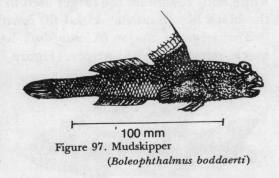

Figure 97. Mudskipper
(*Boleophthalmus boddaerti*)

In shallow waters we often come across sting rays (*Dasyatis*), with their kite-like body continuing into a whip-like tail. (Figure 98.) They are fond of remaining buried in the mud with only their eyes protruding above. In this position they are likely to be accidentally trodden on, and then the tail is lashed from side to side like a whip. One or more spines at the root of the tail, with sawtoothed edges, are equipped with a venom which can give a very painful, nasty wound, sometimes requiring hospitalization.

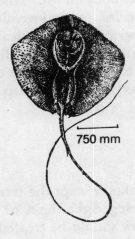

Figure 98. Sting ray (*Dasyatis uarnak*)

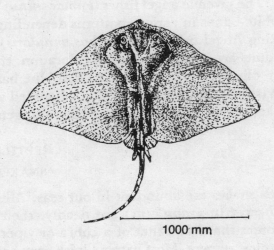

Figure 99. Butterfly ray (*Pleroplatea micrura*)

43

The butterfly ray (*Pteroplatea*) has a very wide body and short tail and grows to a smaller size, but is also venomous. (Figure 99.)

In rock pools we often come across juvenile target perch, sergeant majors, butterfly and angel fishes.

The target perch (*Therapon jarbua*) grows to over 12 cm. (Figure 100.) When seen from above, the design of parallel curved brownish bands on a white body resembles the target used in rifle shooting or archery practice, with the black blotch on the dorsal fin forming the bull's eye.

The sergeant major (*Abudefduf*) has a greenish grey body with straight black, parallel, verical stripes. (Figure 101.) Butterfly fishes (*Chaetodon*) have

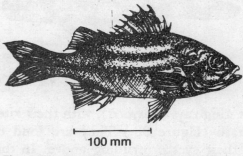

100 mm

Figure 100. Target perch (*Therapon jarbua*)

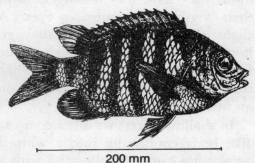

200 mm

Figure 101. Sergeant major (*Abudefduf saxatilis*)

a flat, discoid body with a long snout which is used to poke in crevices of rocks or coral to search for food. Coming in pretty colours, and with their habit of 'flitting' about from place to place, they are aptly named.

The juvenile angel fishes (*Pomacanthus*) have a blue body on which there are white bands in various patterns depending on the species. In the juvenile Blue Ring Angel fish (*Pomacanthus annularis*), they are straight and vertical. The adults are vastly different in coloration; thus the adult blue-ring angel fish has an olive-yellow body with arched blue bands and a blue ring near the cheek. (Plate IV.) Angel fish should be handled with care, as they have a sharp knife-like spine on the gill-cover which also gets entangled in nets.

REPTILIA

SNAKES

Sea snakes are abundant in our seas. All marine snakes (except the estuarine *Chersydrus granulatus*) are deadly, their venom being eight times or more potent than, say, that of a cobra or viper; hence they should be treated with utmost respect. Most have a bluish gray body with darker gray bands on it. The tail is flattened for swimming. Fortunately most sea snakes are mild-tempered and seldom attempt to bite, except the small (60 cm long) *Pelamys platurus*, which can be distinguished by having a body black above and sulphur-yellow below, with the tail blotched with these two colours. (Plate IV.)

TURTLES

Turtles are the sea-cousins of the land tortoises. Their limbs are modified to form flattened paddles which serve them well for swimming, but are useless for walking on land. Females visit sandy beaches to lay clutches of eggs dropped into pits dug in the sand. The eggs are round and white like table tennis balls, about 4 cm in diameter. The eggshell is thin like paper so that the eggs can be dropped without cracking. Up to 180 eggs may be laid at a time. The young hatch out in 1½ to 2 months and immediately crawl off to the sea to swim away.

Four species of turtles are commonly found in our country. The leatherback turtle (*Dermochelys coriacea*) is the largest, growing to 190 cm. (Figure 102.) There are no horny plates (scutes) on the back, which is covered with a smooth leathery skin with seven ridges from neck to tail. This turtle feeds on jellyfish and Portuguese men-of-war. It may mistake plastic bags floating in the sea for its normal prey and swallow them, unfortunately often with fatal results.

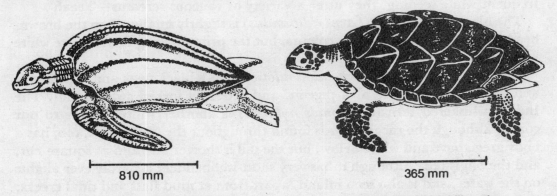

810 mm

365 mm

Figure 102. Leatherback turtle
(*Dermochelys coriacea*)

Figure 103. Hawksbill turtle
(*Eretmochelys imbricata*)

The adult green turtle (*Chelonia mydas*) is a vegetarian, feeding on sea grass and seaweeds. It grows to 140 cm, and, sadly, is in great demand for its delicious meat, and use in turtle soup.

The hawksbill turtle (*Eratmochelys imbricata*) grows to 90 cm. It is easily distinguished from other turtles by its hooked upper jaw and overlapping scutes on the back. (Figure 103.) The beautifully coloured, glossy brown scutes are used for making tortoise-shell curios.

The olive ridley turtle (*Lepidochelys olivacea*) grows to 70 cm, and nests in enormous numbers in winter at night. Some places in Orissa, like Gahirmatha, are well-known nesting sites where up to 200,000 turtles visit the beach in one season.

All turtles are highly endangered species.

AVES*

Some birds are specially suited to life on the sea or coast, while many others are not averse to visiting the seashore for food, although they also frequent tanks, jheels and marshes. (See Plates V – VII for illustrations.)

The brown-headed gull (*Larus brunnicephalus*) is a winter visitor to our coasts, and can be seen in large flocks floating effortlessly on the sea. Its body is a greyish colour above blending to white on the belly, with a greyish-white head. (The brown colour of the head is seen only in summer, when it migrates to Ladakh and Tibet for breeding.) The beak and webbed feet are orange-red. The tips of the first primary feather and outermost nine or ten quills have a conspicuous white patch, seen when the bird is flying. In coastal towns and cities these birds have become scavengers, eating even *pharsan* and *sev-gathia* scattered by religious-minded persons for crows. When squabbling, which is frequent while feeding, they utter a variety of raucous screams—'keeah'.

The black-headed gull (*Larus ridibundus*) is slightly smaller than the brown-headed gull, with similar body colours, but the primary wing feathers are white with black edges and tips.

The gull-billed tern (*Gelochelidon nilotica*) has a black beak and legs, a grey and white body the size of a pigeon, and a deeply forked swallow-tail. The Indian whiskered tern (*Chlidonias hybrida*) is another winter visitor to our coasts, although the race *indica* is found throughout the country. It, too, has a body grey above and white below, but the tail is shorter and almost square-cut, and the bill is red. Although it has very short webbed feet it hardly ever alights on the water, and is also seen inland, apart from at mud flats and tidal creeks, in inundated paddy fields, marshes and jheels.

The little ringed plover (*Charadrius dubius*) is sandy-brown above and white below, with yellow legs, white forehead, and black forecrown and eyes. A white hind-neck collar is followed by a black ring around the neck. It is found on mud flats, shingle banks, sandspits and estuaries, as well as near rivers and tanks. When alarmed, the flock flies twisting and wheeling in unison, uttering a short plaintive whistling cry—'*phiu*'.

---

*The descriptions in this section are adapted from Dr Salim Ali's *Book of Indian Birds*, with the kind permission of the Bombay Natural History Society.

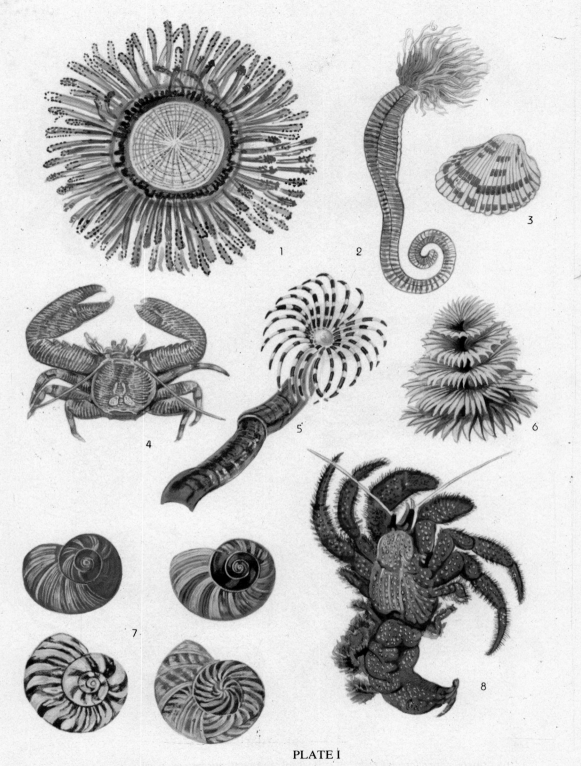

PLATE I

(1) *Porpita pacifica* × 1¹/₂   (2) Burrowing worm (*Amphitrite*) × ¹/₂

(3) False cockle (*Cardita bicolor*) × 1   (4) Porcelain crab (*Petrolisthes boscii*) × 1¹/₂

(5) Feather duster worm (*Potamilla*) × 2   (6) Christmas tree worm × 2

(7) Button-shell (*Umbonium vestiarium*) × 3   (8) Hermit crab (*Dardanus megistos*) × ¹/₂

PLATE II

(1) Box crab *(Calappa lophos)* × 5/8   (2) Bashful crab *(Atergatis integerrimus)* × 1/2
(3) Three-spotted crab *(Portunus sanguinolentus)* × 2/3
(4) Eight-oared swimming crab *(Matuta planipes)* × 1
(5) Cross-and-angels crab *(Charybdis cruciata)* × 1/4   (6) Blue crab *(Portunus pelagicus)* × 1/4

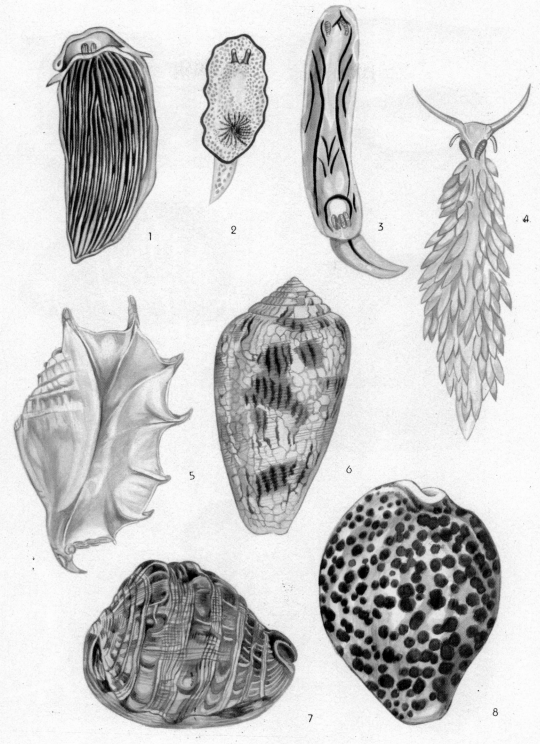

PLATE III

(1) Sea slug *(Pleurophyllidiella paucidentata)* × 6   (2) Sea slug *(Chromodoris tennentana)* × 1¹/₄
(3) Sea slug *(Chromodoris nigrostriata)* × 5   (4) Sea slug *(Aeolis paulinae)* × 3
(5) Scorpion shell *(Lambis lambis)* × ²/₅   (6) Cone shell *(Conus textile)* × ²/₃
(7) Helmet shell *(Cassis rufa)* × ¹/₃   (8) Tiger cowrie *(Cypraea tigris)* × ²/₃

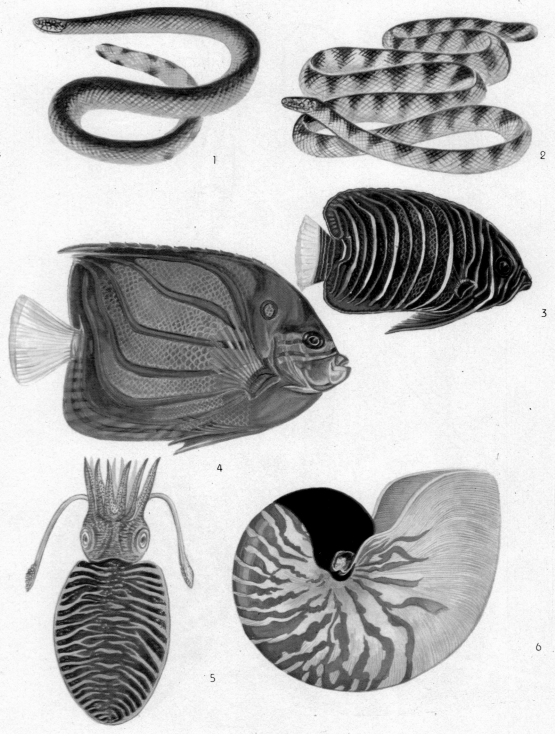

PLATE IV

(1) Yellow-bellied sea snake *(Pelamys platurus)* × ²/₃ (2) Banded sea snake *(Distira cyanocincta)* × ¹/₃
(3) Bluering angel fish (juvenile) *(Pomacanthus annularis)* × 1¹/₄
(4) Bluering angel fish (adult) *(Pomacanthus annularis)* × ¹/₃
(5) Cuttlefish *(Sepia pharaonis)* × ¹/₄ (6) Pearly nautilus *(Nautilus pompilius)* × ¹/₂

PLATE V

(1) Brown-headed gull (*Larus brunnicephalus*) × 1/9   (2) Black-headed gull (*Larus ridibundus*) × 1/8

(3) Gull-billed tern (*Gelochelidon nilotica*) × 1/11   (4) Indian whiskered tern (*Chlidonias hybrida*) × 1/6

(5) Little ringed plover (*Charadrius dubius*) × 1/5   (6) Curlew (*Numenius arquata*) × 1/6

(7) Black-winged stilt (*Himantopus himantopus*) × 1/6   (8) Oyster catcher (*Haematopus ostralegus*) × 1/8

PLATE VI

(1) Common sandpiper *(Tringa hypoleucos)* × ¹/₄   (2) Spotted sandpiper *(Tringa glareola)* × ¹/₄
(3) Redshank *(Tringa totanus)* × ¹/₁₀   (4) Little stint *(Calidris minutus)* × ¹/₅
(5) Fantailed snipe *(Capella gallinago)* × ²/₅   (6) Little cormorant *(Phalacrocorax niger)* × ¹/₁₀
(7) Spoonbill *(Platalea leucorodia)* × ¹/₉   (8) Flamingo *(Phoenicopterus roseus)* × ¹/₁₅

PLATE VII

(1) Indian reef heron *(Egretta gularis)* × ¹/₁₀   (2) Little green bittern *(Butorides striatus)* × ¹/₇

(3) Night heron *(Nycticorax nycticorax)* × ¹/₁₀   (4) White-bellied sea eagle *(Haliaeetus leucogaster)* × ¹/₁₀

(5) Pied kingfisher *(Ceryle rudis)* × ¹/₅   (6) Black-capped kingfisher *(Halcyon pileata)* × ¹/₃

(7) White-breasted kingfisher *(Halcyon smyrnensis)* × ¹/₃

(8) Brown-headed stork-billed kingfisher *(Pelargopsis capensis)* × ¹/₆

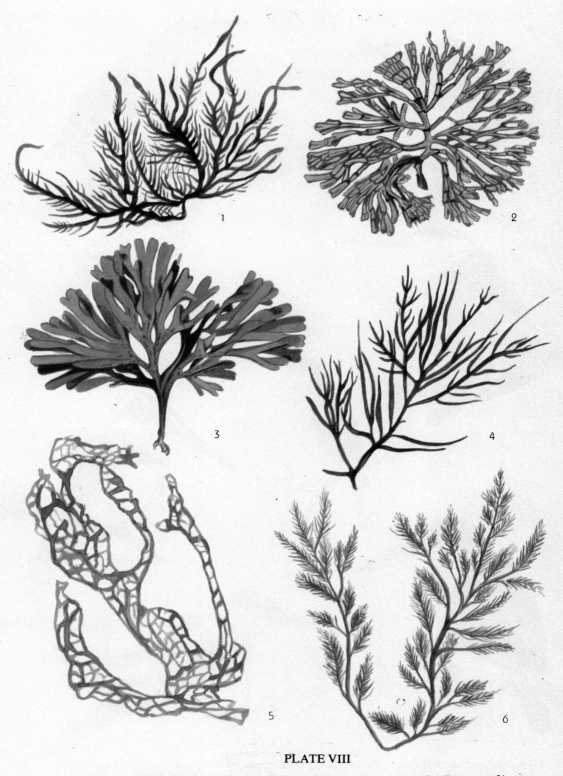

PLATE VIII

(1) *Grateloupia filicina* (Wulfen) C. Ag. × ¹/₂   (2) *Amphiroa anceps* (Lamk.) Descne × ²/₃
(3) *Stoechospermum marginatum* (Ag.) Kutz × ¹/₄   (4) *Solieria robusta* (Grcv.) Kylin × ²/₅
(5) *Ulva reticulata* Forsk. × ³/₅   (6) *Acanthophora delilei* Lamour × ²/₃

The black-winged stilt (*Himantopus himantopus*) is a lanky black, greyish-brown and white wading bird, with slender reddish legs 25 cm long, and a thin straight black bill. It is found near salt pans and tidal mud flats. When alarmed and flying away it utters a squeaky piping 'chek-chek-chek'.

The curlew (*Numenius arquata*) has a sandy-brown body streaked with black and fulvous. The rump and lower back are white. It is of the size of a hen, but has a long, slender down-curved beak, 15 cm long. It runs along the seashore at the water's edge, probing into soft mud for snails and crustaceans, and also feeds on seaweeds. While flying, it utters a shrill, plaintive 'coor-lee' (or cur-lew). The whimbrel (*Numenius phaeopus*), a winter visitor and smaller cousin of the curlew, is distinguished by the white stripe (centre parting) in the middle of the dark crown of the head and by white eyebrows, as well as by its musical cry 'tetti-tet'.

The common sandpiper (*Tringa hypoleucos*) is greyish-brown above, white below, with a pale dusky breast and a few dark streaks on the foreneck. During flight, the brown rump and tail with white outer feathers is prominent. Found on rocky seashores and tidal creeks, its cry is a pretty, long-drawn, trilly 'wheeit, wheeit', or a shrill, piping 'tee-tee-tee'.

The spotted sandpiper (*Tringa glareola*), a small bird the size of a quail, is brown, with indistinct white spots above, and with a white rump and lower back. There is a white stripe from the beak to the nape of the neck passing above the eye. It is a wading bird found on tidal mud flats, as well as in marshes and flooded paddy fields. The alarm call is a shrill 'chiff-chiff-chiff'.

The redshank (*Tringa totanus*) is also greyish-brown above and white below, with the white breast finely streaked with brown. When flying, the red legs trail behind, and the brown-barred white tail is conspicuous. The cry is a shrill, piping 'tiu-tiu-tiu'. It is found near estuaries and jheels.

The little stint (*Calidris minutus*) is again mottled greyish-brown or dusky above and white below, with blackish beak and legs. The rump and middle tail feathers are dark brown, outer tail feathers smoky-brown. During flight, a faint, narrow white bar on the pointed wings can be seen. Wading on tidal mud flats, its cry is a soft musical 'wit-wit-wit' or a low 'tr-rr'.

The fan-tailed snipe (*Capella gallinago*) is dark brown, streaked with black, rufous and buff above, white below, with a thin straight beak 6 cm long. It is a winter visitor to tidal creeks.

The little cormorant (*Phalacrocorax niger*) is a black bird with a long stiff tail, the size of a duck. The thin bill is sharply hooked at its tip. Found on tidal creeks and brackish water lagoons, it swims and catches fish underwater, and then basks in the sun with outstretched wings.

The spoonbill (*Platalea leucorodia*) is a long-legged, long-necked, duck-shaped, white bird with black legs, and a black and yellow spoon-shaped beak. There is a pale yellowish-brown patch on the foreneck. It feeds in the morning and evening by sweeping its beak from side to side in estuarine mud flats as well as river banks and jheels. Flocks fly in a V-formation or in a diagonal line.

The Indian reef heron (*Egretta gularis*) is found on our western coast. It may be completely white or slaty-blue with a white patch on the throat. It wades in the surf looking for mud-skippers, snails and crustaceans.

The paddy bird or pond heron (*Ardeola grayii*), despite its name, also frequents tidal mud flats and mangrove swamps, wading for fish and crabs. When disturbed, it utters a harsh croak.

The little green bittern (*Butorides striatus*) is blackish-grey and dark bronze-green above, and ash-grey below. The crown of the head is shining greenish-black, while the chin and throat are white. Found at tidal creeks and mangrove swamps, it is active at dawn and dusk, and on cloudy overcast days.

The night heron (*Nycticorax nycticorax*) is ashy-grey above with a shining black back, and white below. The crown of the head and nape are black. Found in the same environment as the bittern, it, too, is active at dusk and night. Its cry is a loud, raucous '*kwaark*'.

The oyster catcher (*Haematopus ostralegus*) is black above and white below, with red beak and legs. It runs about at low tide on rocky shores and tidal estuaries and prises open oysters and mussels, and also digs out worms and crabs from the sand.

The white-bellied sea eagle (*Haliaeetus leucogaster*) is brown above, with white belly, head and neck. The end of the wedge-shaped tail is also white. It feeds on fishes and sea snakes, and a pair may be found in the same area for years. The call is a loud, nasal, cackling '*keuk-keuk*'.

Then, we have the kingfishers. They, too, are not purely marine, also commonly frequenting streams, jheels and tanks. The pied kingfisher (*Ceryle rudis*), found at tidal creeks, has a speckled black and white body with a stout, straight, dagger-like beak. It hovers at the same place for quite some time until it sees a fish, when it dives in. Its call is a sharp '*chirruk*'.

The white-breasted kingfisher (*Halcyon smyrnensis*) has a glistening turquoise-blue body with chocolate-brown head, neck and belly, and a white breast. The strong beak is red. Also found near the shore, it gives out a loud, repeated chattering call while perched on a tree.

The black-capped kingfisher (*Halcyon pileata*) is cobalt blue above, pale rust below, with a velvet black head and white collar, and a red back. Its favourite haunt is mangrove swamps bordering tidal creeks.

The body of the brown-headed stork-billed kingfisher (*Pelargopsis capensis*) is a pale greenish-blue above, and pale yellowish-brown below. It is larger than other kingfishers and also has a bigger red beak. It is found in tidal creeks overgrown with mangroves and screw pine. It does not hover; its call is a raucous, chattering, explosive '*Ke-ke-ke-ke-ke*'.

The Flamingo (*Phoenicoptreus reseus*) is a long-legged bird with a rosy white body and scarlet wings bordered with black. The pink bill is abruptly bent downward in the middle. It is found at *jheels,* tidal mud flats, lagoons, estuaries and salt pans where it feeds by submerging its head in shallw water; the inverted beak scrapes the bottom mud, which is strained by the bill to separate crustaceans, worms, insects and seeds of marsh plants.

Although the size of a goose, the flamingo stands 1.2 m tall. Its call is a goose-like honk but, while feeding, the flock constantly babbles. The nest is a conical mound of mud 15 to 30 cm high. Flamingoes nest in vast colonies.

Unlike most land birds, which help us by ridding insect and rodent pests which devastate our crops, the birds described above *seem* to serve no useful purpose. In fact, as some of them feed on fish, crabs, oysters and clams, we would tend to believe that they apparently compete with man for food. But the size of their prey is so small that it rarely serves as food for us. And others, like the curlew, golden plover (*Pluvialis dominica*) and black-tailed godwit (*Limosa limosa*), because of their wariness and swift flight, as also their tasty flesh, are hunted for sport.

Many sea birds are found in immense numbers at their favourite roosting sites. Their droppings, called guano, are excellent source of nitrogen and phosphorus, and used as manure.

Cormorants are trained in China and Japan to catch fish, which are then appropriated by the fisherman who looks after the birds.

Some swifts (*Collocalia*) use their sticky saliva to build nests. They breed in vast colonies in grottoes on some rocky islands off the Konkan coast and some islands of the Andaman group. The nests are esteemed by the Chinese as an epicurean delicacy, and fetch a high price.

FLOTSAM AND JETSAM

The terms above are meant to include material from a shipwreck (or thrown overboard) and found, respectively, floating or sunk in the sea. For our purposes, however, they concern live animals (and plants) normally swimming, or floating, in the sea, sometimes washed ashore and found lying there alive or dead, usually as a result of storms or onshore winds.

Foremost in this category come four kinds of coelenterates, viz. *Porpita*, *Velella* (by-the-wind sailor), *Physalia* (Portuguese man-of-war or bluebottle) and jellyfish. All of these are found, sometimes in large numbers, washed up on sandy beaches prior to the monsoon.

Porpita has no common name. (Plate I.) It consists of a flat, circular, disc-like float of a beautiful, iridescent, deep blue colour and ranges in size from a 25-paise coin to a rupee coin. The central float is surrounded by whorls of dark blue tentacles. However, if the animal has been lying on the shore for some time, these tentacles will have decayed, leaving only the central disc. The by-the-wind sailor (*Velella*) is similar but has, in addition, a vertical 'sail' on top of the float, which enables it to be blown swiftly before the wind. (Figure 104.) Both the animals are harmless.

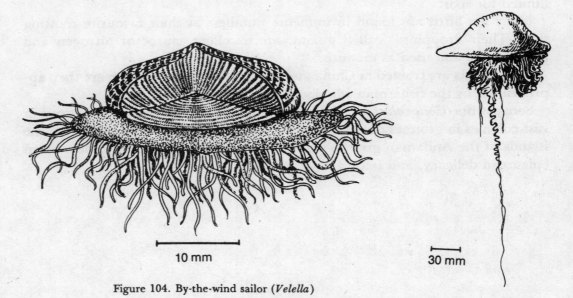

10 mm

30 mm

Figure 104. By-the-wind sailor (*Velella*)

Figure 105. Portuguese man-of-war
(*Physalia utriculus*)

50

The Portuguese man-of-war (*Physalia*) has a transparent blue grape-like float, from below which spring one long and numerous short tentacles, (Figure 105.) These tentacles are extremely retractile, and can be extended for many centimetres below the float or contracted close to it. They are equipped with batteries of stinging cells which, in the larger Pacific Ocean forms, can even kill a man. Fortunately, the type found in Indian seas rarely has a float over 4 cm long. Still, it can 'sting' badly. Never, therefore, handle it with bare hands, but use forceps.

Many kinds of jellyfishes live in our seas, but the type most commonly found washed ashore has its 'bell' ranging from 10 cm to over 65 cm. Through the translucent colourless body, which resembles the fruit of the palmyra palm (*tadgola*) in colour as well as consistency, can be seen the four orange, horseshoe-shaped reproductive organs. The tentacles hang from four branched, palmate (hand-shaped) extensions of the bell. (See Figure 5.)

Very rarely, you may come across a piece of driftwood, an empty bottle, or even a rubber 'chappal' to which are attached goose barnacles (*Lepas*). (Figure 106.) A soft stalk with several white limy plates is attached to the substrate which is always floating. These animals are so named because people in olden days believed that geese grew from them!

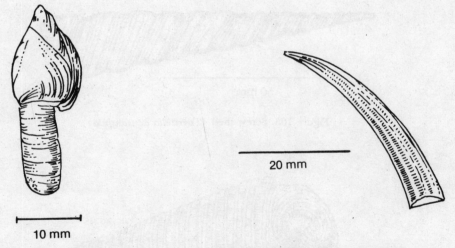

10 mm

20 mm

Figure 106. Goose barnacle (*Lepas*)   Figure 107. Elephant-tusk shell (*Dentalium*)

Sometimes, while walking on the beach, you will come across a lobster or a crab lying sprawling on the sand or mud. Even when you approach it, it does not try to run away. It is only when you pick it up that you realize the reason why it did not escape. It is the empty 'moult' cast off by a growing animal. These animals are encased in a hard, unyielding armour-like shell, which cannot grow in size as our skin does. Hence the process of moulting; at this time the animal casts off its shell. Afterwards it is very soft; it takes in a lot of water and swells up in size. After a few days a new shell hardens, and the animal has to wait some weeks or even months before it can moult again.

Washed ashore on sandy beaches, you will come across many kinds of sea shells. These animals live in depths below the inter-tidal zone, so that you will hardly ever come across the living animals except by diving.

The elephant-tusk shells (*Dentalium*) are very appropirately named, as they have a slightly curved tubular shell with one end larger than the other. (Figure 107.) The animal lives inside the tube and is partly buried in sand, with the pointed end upward, from which water is taken in for breathing. It grows to less than 4 cm long and lives in shallow water, only the dead shells being found washed up on beaches.

Auger or screw-shells (*Turritella*) should be distinguished from the similarly shaped but much smaller *Potamides* or *Telescopium* (horn-shells) (Figures 108 and 109 respectively.) Both are long and tapering, but the screw-shell has a thin and simple mouth without the thickened or everted lip of the horn-shell. Moreover, the spires of the screw-shell have only ridges but no tubercles. The shell grows to 10 cm in length.

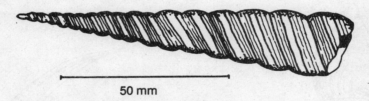

50 mm

Figure 108. Screw-shell (*Turritella acutangula*)

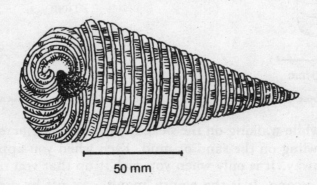

50 mm

Figure 109. Horn-shell (*Telescopium telescopium*)

The wing-shell (*Strombus*) has its shell mouth widened into a 'wing' with a thick border. (Figure 110.) Under the dark brown outermost layer, the shell is white. By etching selected areas with acid, interesting designs can be made on the shell; along with the cowrie, this shell is therefore used by craftsmen near Rameswaram to make cameos.

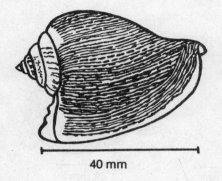

40 mm

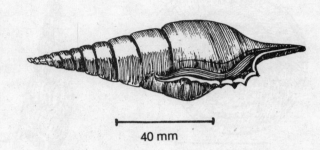

40 mm

Figure 110. Wing-shell (*Strombus*)

Figure 111. Beak-shell (*Tibia curta*)

The scorpion-shell (*Lambis lambis*) grows to 18 cm in length and has five long finger-like processes flanking the lip with one more along the apex of the spire. A related form (*Lambis chiragra*) from Lakshadweep has curved 'fingers' placed equidistantly along the sides of the shell. (Plate III.)

The beak-shell (*Tibia curta*) has a long tapering spiral shell with several short blunt spines along the flared mouth and a longer tubular 'beak' at the front end of the mouth whorl. (Figure 111.)

The carrier-shell (*Xenophora*) has a conical shell like *Trochus*, but is broader and less high. (Figure 112.) It camouflages itself by cementing small dead shells on the whorls of its shell.

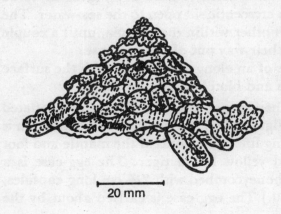

Figure 112. Carrier-shell (*Xenophora*)

20 mm

Similar in shape are the staircase shells (*Architectonica*). The projecting inner edges of the whorls seen on the sides of the umbilicus have a fanciful resemblance to a spiral staircase. (Figure 113.)

The wentle-trap (*Epitonium*) has a long *Turritella*-type shell but has beautifully ridged ribs along the whorls. (Figure 114.)

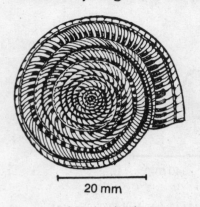

20 mm

Figure 113. Staircase shell or sundial
shell (*Architectonica*)

Figure 114. Wentle-trap
(*Epitonium*)

15 mm

40 mm

Figure 115. Tun-shell
(*Tonna dolium*)

Helmet shells (*Cassis*) are the largest and heaviest of our shells, large specimens weighing more than a kilogram. Here too the shell consists of differently coloured layers, and is used for cameo-work. (Plate III.)

The tun-shell (*Tonna dolium*) is, on the contrary, very light in weight, having a very thin globose shell. (Figure 115.)

The sacred chank (*Xancus pyrum*), with its white fusiform shell with three or four columnar ridges, is well known in legend and folklore. (Figure 116.) Bangles made from it are a 'must' for every Bengali bride. The egg capsules are laid in a loose spiral shaped like a ram's horn. (Figure 117.) Over 25 to 30 capsules form an egg case; each has a crescentic slit open to the sea-water. The young are cannibalistic, and eat each other within the capsule, until a couple of hundred remain, which then eat their way out of the egg-case.

Mitre-shells (*Mitra*) have the shape of an elongated spindle with the surface ornamented with spiral rows of spots and blotches. (Figure 118.)

The melon- or bailer-shell (*Melo*) has its mouth whorl so large and inflated that the spire of the shell is hidden. (Figure 119.) The shell, growing to 20 cm is a pale orange-red, but is hidden during life by the folds of the mantle and foot which are prettily striped black and yellow like a tiger. The egg-case is a gigantic 30 cm high glassy cylinder, honeycombed with 2½ cm long capsules, looking like a pineapple. (Figure 120.) The egg-case is carried about by the

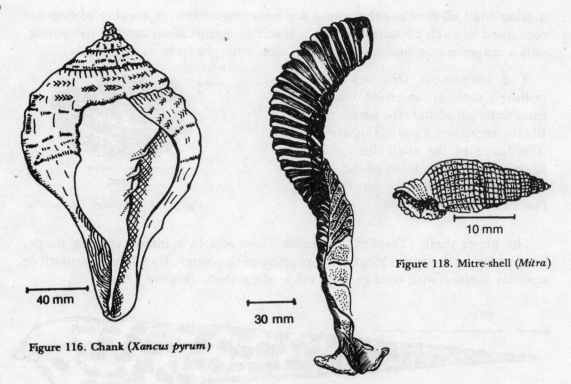

Figure 116. Chank (*Xancus pyrum*)

Figure 117. Egg mass of chank

Figure 118. Mitre-shell (*Mitra*)

10 mm

40 mm

30 mm

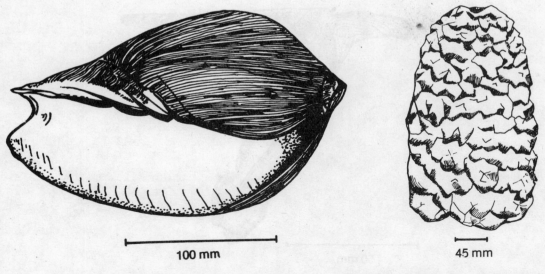

100 mm

Figure 119. Melon-shell (*Melo*)

45 mm

Figure 120. Egg mass of melon-shell

mother snail all the time the young are brooding within. A number of eggs are contained in each capsule, but, as a result of cannibalism among the young, only a single young one, over 2 cm in size, emerges from each capsule.

The harp-shells (*Harpa*) have a polished shell ornamented with prominent longitudinal ribs which resemble the strings of a harp. (Figure 121.) The lustre of the shell during life is maintained by the lobes of the mantle covering the shell as in *Cypraea*, *Natica*, *Oliva*, *Melo*, etc.

50 mm

Figure 121. Harp-shell (*Harpa*)

The auger-shells (*Terebra*) resemble *Turritella* in a long, tapering shape, but instead of the spiral ridged sculpturing of the latter, they have a smooth or nodular surface with orange spots on a white shell. (Figure 122.)

50 mm

Figure 122. Auger-shell (*Terebra*)

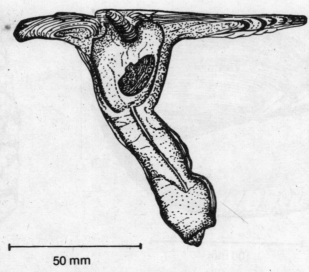

50 mm

Figure 123. One valve of a hammer oyster (*Malleus*)

56

The hammer oyster (*Malleus*) is an anachronism in bivalve shells. Its dark, misshapen, corrugated shell is shaped like the letter 'T'; the 'ears' present on both sides of the hinge in scallops and wing-shells, here form the top of the 'T'. (Figure 123.) During life a thick crust of sponges, hydroids, bryozoa and ascidians grow on the shell, thus camouflaging it.

The thorny cockle (*Spondylus*) behaves more like the edible oyster in that the right (lower) valve is cemented to rocks. Both the valves have long spines, and are very conspicuous because of their bright yellow or red colour. (Figure 124.)

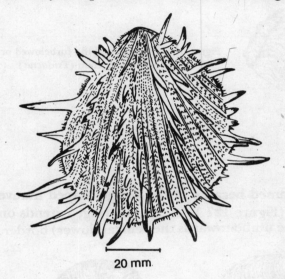

20 mm

Figure 124. One valve of the thorny cockle
(*Spondylus*)

The pen-shell (*Pinna*) lives partly buried in sand and has large (over 30 cm long) wedge-shaped valves. (Figure 125.) Like the mussel, it spins silky byssus threads, which can be made into cloth of superb quality.

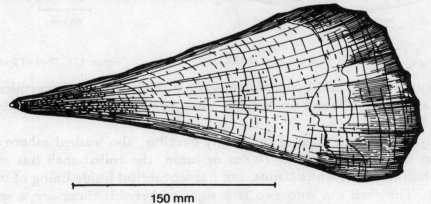

150 mm
Figure 125. One valve of a pen-shell (*Pinna*)

The furbelowed or holy-water clam (*Tridacna*) is a gigantic relative of the oyster. Some species grow to over 225 kg. (Figure 126.) Its valves were used as baptismal fonts in churches. The clam lives vertically buried among coral reefs. The mantle has iridescent orange, blue or purple frills, and there are algae living within the animal, so the clam basks in the sun with its shell agape to let these algae carry out photosynthesis.

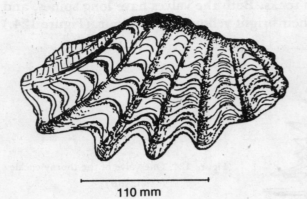

Figure 126. One valve of the furbelowed or holy-water clam (*Tridacna*)

110 mm

The sunset shell (*Siliqua*) is so named because of the wedge-shaped mauve bands on the narrow smooth shell. (Figure 127.) An oblique ridge extends on the *inner* facies of the valves from the umbo towards the ventral (lower) border.

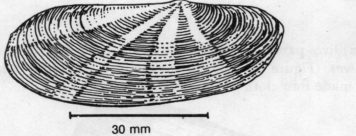

30 mm

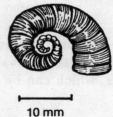

10 mm

Figure 127. One valve of sunset shell (*Siliqua*)   Figure 128. Shell of *Spirula*

The internal shell of the cephalopod *Spirula*, looking like a 6 cm coiled ram's horn, can often be found on beaches when continuous onshore winds blow. (Figure 128.)

Finally we have the shell of the pearly nautilus, also washed ashore during monsoon storms. Growing to 10 cm or more, the coiled shell has external brownish orange and white bands, but has a beautiful inside lining of mother-of-pearl. The shell cut into two is a sight to behold; there are a series of gradually enlarging chambers separated by partitions but connected by a

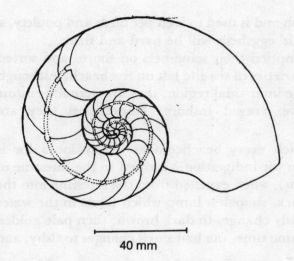

40 mm

narrow tube in each partition. The animal lives only in the last (and biggest) chamber; the other chambers are filled with a gas secreted by the animal, which enables it to float. (Figure 129 and Plate IV.)

Several kinds of egg-cases of molluscs can be seen on mud flats or sandy beaches. In winter one often comes across macaroni-like irregularly coiled yellow strings. These are laid by the sea hares (*Aplysia*, *Notarchus*). (See Figure 66.) Then we may see flat, brittle, horseshoe-shaped, muddy brown 'sand collars' about 10 cm across. These are the egg-cases of the moon snail (*Natica*). (See Figure 55.)

Occasionally on beaches we may see a hard, chalk-white, shield-shaped object, on the surface of which are finely etched wavy lines, and at one end a sharp spine. (Figure 130.) It may be up to 15 cm long. This is the shell, called 'pen', of the cuttlefish and is also locally called 'sea foam'. The shell is hidden

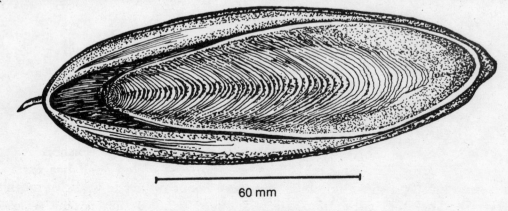

60 mm

Figure 130. Cuttlebone

59

inside the body of the live cuttlefish and is used to feed pet birds and poultry, a source of calcium so that the birds' eggshells will be hard and firm.

Often, after fishermen have emptied their seine-nets on shore, and sorted their catch, you may find many varieties of sea-life left on the beach. Although these may have been caught in the inter-tidal region, they are actually visitors from deeper waters which have strayed inshore. Nonetheless they are interesting to collect.

One item among flotsam which every beachcomber avidly looks for is ambergris. A product of digestion (or indigestion?) formed in the intestine of the sperm whale (*Physeter catodon*), when expelled from the intestine into the sea it is a sticky, dark, almost black, shapeless lump which floats in the water and smells abominably. It gradually changes to dark brown, then pale golden and finally chalky white. At the same time, the bad smell changes to fishy, and then to a sweetish musky odour.

Ambergris is used in the most expensive perfumes to 'fix' the fragrance. While perfumes prepared without it lose their fragrance within days, those made with it will last for months.

In olden days, ambergris was worth its weight in gold. In 1956, a piece weighing 69 kg fetched US $ 20,000. One of the largest known pieces was a lump 1.65 metres long, 76 cm in diameter and weighing 420 kg; it came from a 15-metre-long sperm whale.

PLANTS

Three major groups of plants are found at the seashore: seaweeds or algae, mangroves, and sand binders. (See Plate VIII for illustrations.)

SEAWEEDS

Also known as algae, seaweeds are primitive plants without differentiation into roots, stem or leaves, and they do not have flowers. They are attached to rocks under water by branched *holdfasts*, but can survive exposure to air for short periods in the intertidal zone. The vegetative part above the holdfast is called the *thallus*. The thallus may be in the form of a simple thread, a branched filament, a hollow tube or bladder, a bushy tuft of cylindrical or flattened branches, or of a simple or compound blade.

From the pigments in their tissues, algae are divided into blue-green, green, brown and red. As we go from shallow to deep water, we generally find first the green, then brown and finally the red algae, with a wide degree of overlapping.

Blue-green algae are the most primitive among seaweeds. Their colour is due to a water-soluble pigment called phycocyanin. They are inconspicuous, being just a filament made up of a chain or shapeless mass of cells surrounded by a slimy sheath. *Hyella*, a typical representative, occurs as tiny patches of horizontally creeping, gelatinous filaments 100 to 200 microns long (a micron is

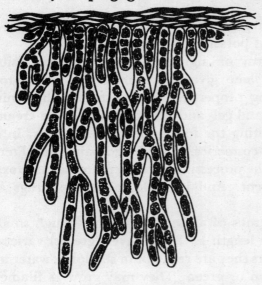

Figure 131. *Hyella* —a blue-green alga

0.1 mm

61

a thousandth part of a millimetre) on snail shells, barnacles and corals. From these surface filaments arise perforating filaments which bore into the shell. (Figure 131.)

Many blue-green algae show remarkable variability, existing in different forms and shapes. Thus *Hyella* is now thought to be only a phase in the development of a blue-green alga called *Entophysalis*.

Green seaweeds appear green because of the green pigment chlorophyll, which helps to manufacture food in the presence of sunlight. They have different body shapes. (Figure 132.) Thus the sea lettuce (*Ulva*) has flat, sheet-like thalli, *Enteromorpha* is tubular, while *Codium* may be filamentous. *Caulerpa* has feathery thalli and can grow on a sandy bottom as a carpet over 10 cm thick. Some green algae (e.g. *Halimeda*) become encrusted with lime.

Brown seaweeds have the green pigment chlorophyll, but the green colour is masked by the yellow and brown pigments xanthophyll, carotin and fucoxanthin. Like the green seaweeds, brown seaweeds may exhibit a variety of shapes, ranging from minute, delicate, filamentous branches (as in *Ectocarpus*) to coarse, hollow, sausage-like chains 30 cm or more in length, or short-stalked forms with broad thalli some of which may be two metres broad, many-branched forms, and the giant kelps of the Pacific Ocean, some of which may be 35 metres long and form veritable underwater forests. (Figure 133.)

The thalli of gulf weed (*Sargassum*) look remarkably like leaves. This plant also has small, air-filled bladders which help it to float when it is torn away by waves.

Brown seaweeds are used for manuring feeds, as fodder for cattle, sheep, goats and pigs, and for extraction of potash and iodine.

Algin (alginic acid), in the form of alginates of sodium, potassium, ammonium, calcium and of propylene glycol, are extracted from brown seaweeds. Algin has water-absorbing properties and is used for thickening, suspending, stabilizing, emulsifying and gel- and film-forming. In ice-cream it imparts a smooth texture by preventing the formation of ice crystals. In car polishes it suspends the abrasives. In cosmetics, water-based paints and French dressings it acts as an emulsifier. In the processing of rubber latex and in textile printing it acts as a stabilizing agent. And it is also added to drugs and antibiotics.

Red seaweeds are the most numerous of all seaweeds and, though smaller than the brown seaweeds (maximum length 1 − 2 m), have a greater variety of shapes. (Figure 134.) In deeper waters they are red, but in shallower water may appear purple, violet, or even brown or green. They may grow as filaments attached to plants, as thin films on stones, and as large, fleshy or membranous forms. Thus the sea mosses, like *Polysiphonia*, are branched filaments, while

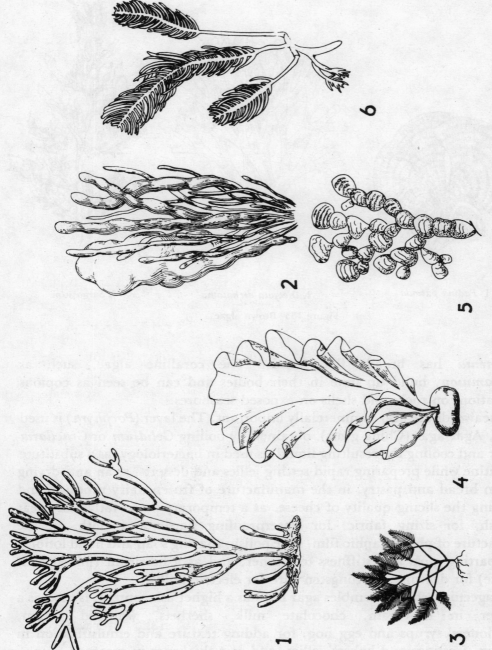

1. *Codium tomentosum* 2. *Enteromorpha intestinalis* 3. *Bryopsis* 4. *Ulva lactuca* 5. *Halimeda* 6. *Caulerpa*

Figure 132. Green algae

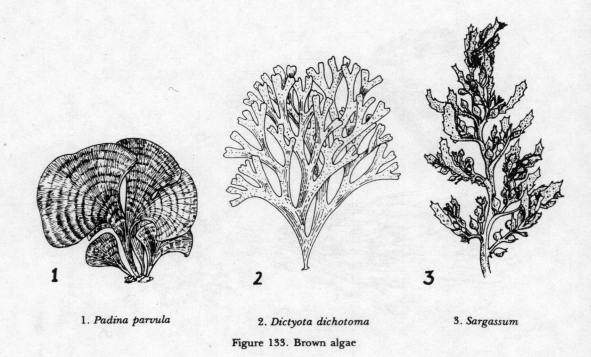

1. *Padina parvula*   2. *Dictyota dichotoma*   3. *Sargassum*

Figure 133. Brown algae

Rhodymenia has broad, flat fronds. The coralline algae, such as *Lithothamnion*, build up lime in their bodies and can be seen as copious encrustations on rocks and shells on exposed seashores.

Red seaweeds are also commercially important. The laver (*Porphyra*) is used as food, Agar-agar (China grass), obtained by boiling *Gelidium* or *Gracilaria* in water and cooling the resulting liquid, is used in bacteriology, as a substitute for gelatine while preparing rapid-setting jellies and desserts, as an anti-drying agent in bread and pastry, in the manufacture of frozen dairy products and improving the slicing quality of cheese, as a temporary preservative for meat and fish, for sizing fabric, for waterproofing paper and cloth, in the manufacture of photographic film, shoe polish, shaving soap and hand lotions, for imparting gloss and stiffness to leather, and as a lubricant (mixed with graphite) for drawing hot tungsten wire for electric bulbs.

Carrageenin, which resembles agar but has a higher ash content, is used as a stabilizer in ice-cream, chocolate milk, sherbets, whipped cream, confectioners' syrups and egg nog, for adding texture and emulsification in puddings, frostings and bakers' jellies, and as a thickener in creamed soups.

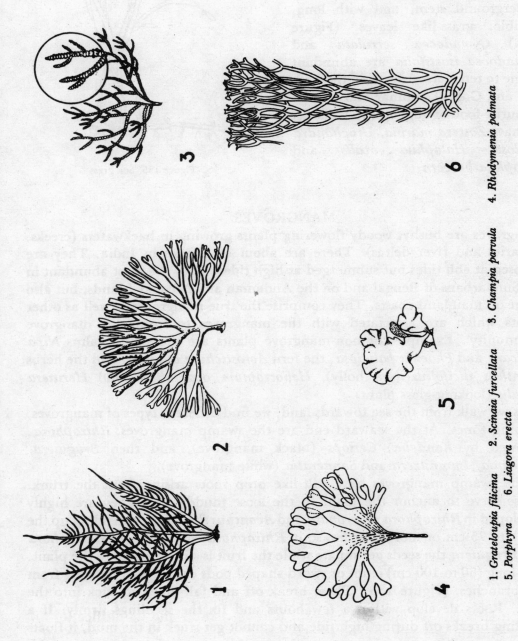

1. Grateloupia filicina   2. Scinaia furcellata   3. Champia parvula   4. Rhodymenia palmata

5. Porphyra   6. Liagora erecta

Figure 134. Red algae

The sea grasses are flowering plants with true roots attached to an underground stem, and with long, flexible, grass-like leaves. (Figure 135.) *Cymadocea serrulata* and *Cymadocea isoetifolia* are abundant at one to ten metres' depth in the Palk Bay and Gulf of Mannar and are the favourite food of dugongs. In Gujarat, we have *Zostera marina*, *Urochondra setulosa*, *Halophila ovalis* and *Halophila beccerii*.

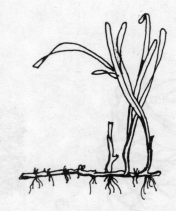

Figure 135. Sea grass

MANGROVES

Mangroves are bushy, woody flowering plants growing in backwaters (creeks, estuaries and river deltas). There are about 45 species in India. They are exposed at ebb tides but submerged at high tides. They are most abundant in the Sundarbans of Bengal and on the Andaman and Nicobar Islands, but also occur on mainland coasts. They comprise the true mangroves as well as other plants which are associated with the mangroves to form the 'mangrove community'. Examples of non-mangrove plants are the saline palms *Nipa fruticans* and *Phoenix paludosa*, the fern *Acrostichum aureum*, and the herbs *Acanthus ilicifolius* (sea holly), *Heliotropium ovalifolium* and *Heritiera litoralis* (looking-glass plant).

As we walk from the sea towards land, we find different types of mangroves, forming zones. At the seaward end are the swamp mangroves, *Rhizophora*, followed by *Kandelia*, *Ceriops* (black mangrove), and then *Bruguiera*, *Avicennia*, *Lumnitzera* and *Sonneratia* (white mangrove).

The swamp mangroves have stilt-like prop roots arising from the trunk. These serve to anchor the plant in the loose muddy soil. They are highly developed in *Rhizophora mucronata* and *Acanthus ilicifolius*, extending up the trunk to 75 cm or more, but less so in *Rhizophora conjugata*. In *Rhizophora* and *Bruguiera* the seeds germinate while the fruit is still attached to the plant. The long (50 to 100 cm) club- or sword-shaped pods can be seen hanging from the branches. (Figure 136.) These break off and fall down to stick into the mud. Roots develop within a few hours and fix the seedlings firmly. If a seedling breaks off during high tide and cannot get stuck in the mud, it floats vertically until it gets a chance to wedge itself into a crack in the mud at ebb tide.

Figure 136. Hanging seed of mangrove

Figure 137. Breathing roots of mangrove

In *Bruguiera*, the horizontal parent roots bend out of the mud into knee-like structures. In *Avicennia, Sonneratia, Ceriops*, etc. the underground lateral roots give out root branches which grow vertically to come out of the mud for a height of 10 cm (in *Avicennia*) or as much as 50 cm (in *Sonneratia*). (Figure 137.) These breathing roots have tiny pores which take in air to supply oxygen to the underground roots, which would otherwise suffocate in the poorly aerated mud.

By breaking the force of waves and trapping silt particles, mangroves help to prevent coastal erosion and create land from the sea. First the true mangroves (*Avicennia*) settle down, followed by other mangroves such as *Rhizophora, Bruguiera, Ceriops*, etc. forming the mixed mangrove forests. As the ground level rises, the mangroves are replaced by shore plants like *Aegiceras* and *Excoecaria*. These are followed by salt-tolerant grasses such as *Myriostachya, Oryza sativa* var. *patnai* and *achra*, and *Oryza coarctata* (wild rice).

The tissues of mangroves contain tannin which is used in the leather industry for tanning. The wood is burnt for fuel while the leaves serve as camel fodder.

SAND BINDERS

Farther up the shore, in dry sand we find many prostrate (i.e. lying horizontally on the sand) and erect plants which help to bind the sand and prevent it from being blown away by the wind. They have thick, fleshy leaves for storing water. In some, the leaves are reduced in size so as to lessen the loss of water from their surface; instead, the green stems help to carry out photosynthesis. Calcium

67

oxalate crystals form within their tissues; these scatter light so as to maximize photosynthesis. All are flowering plants.

Typical examples of prostrate sand binders are *Arthrocnemum indicum, Atriplex stocksii, Ipomoea pes caprae* (goat's foot), *Sesuvium portulacastrum,* and *Suaeda nudiflora,* while *Salicornia brachiata, Spinifex squarrosus* and *Suaeda maritima* are erect. (Figures 138 and 139.)

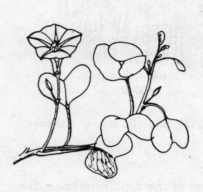

Figure 138. A runner of goat's foot (*Ipomoea pes caprae*), showing leaves and flowers

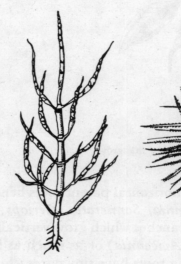

Figure 139. *Salicornia* plant

Figure 140. Fruit mass of *Spinifex squarrosus*

In *Salsola foetida*, the minute flowers smell of rotten fish.

In *Spinifex squarrosus* the hairy, ball-like collection of minute fruits breaks off from the plant and rolls about on the sand with the wind. (Figure 140.) As it rolls about, the fruits drop off one by one. Because of the rolling on the sand, the bristles wear off and the remaining cluster of fruits gets buried in the sand.

GLOSSARY

(Terms in the explanations which have been separately defined are italicized)

Abdomen: rear region of body in crustaceans.

Anterior: forward of; in front of; nearer the head.

Appendage: an organ or part attached to the body.

Autotomy: self-mutilation by loss of limbs (in crustaceans), or arms (in brittle stars).

Berry: mass of eggs carried under the abdomen by female crustaceans.

Byssus: tough horny threads used for attachment to rocks by mussels.

Carapace: shield covering the back of certain animals (e.g. crustaceans, turtles).

Cephalothorax: the body-region formed by fusion of head and *thorax*.

Chitin: horny substance forming the outer cuticle of crustaceans.

Chlorophyll: green colouring matter of plants, used for *photosynthesis*.

Cilia: minute, rapidly vibrating, short hairs present on or in the body of many animals.

Commensal: an organism living with another and sharing the food, both species as a rule benefiting by the association.

Compressed: flattened from side to side.

Depressed: flattened from top to bottom.

Detritus: particles produced by breakdown of animal and plant bodies.

Dorsal: pertaining to the back.

Euryhaline: capable of living in waters of varying salinities.

Faeces: excrement from gut.

Filament: a slender or thread-like structure.

Flagellum: minute, whip-like, long hair found on or in many animals (such as sponges.)

Flotsam: floating wreckage.

Gills: organs for breathing in water.

Halophyte: plant able to live where the soil is impregnated with salt.

Hermaphrodite: organism with both male and female reproductive organs.

Hirsute: covered with hair.

Holdfast: the sucker or disc on the *thallus* of some algae.

Hydrotheca: a cup-like structure into which a coelenterate *polype* can withdraw.

Invertebrate: backboneless animal.

Jetsam: goods or cargo thrown overboard in dire need (usually during a storm) to lighten a ship.

Lateral: at or toward the side.

Mantle: outer soft fold of skin next to shell of molluscs.

Median: pertaining to the middle; situated on the lengthwise centre-line along the back or belly.

Metamorphosis: striking change in form undergone by some animals during development.

Micron: one-thousandth part of a millimetre.

Moult: (verb) to cast or shed periodically the skin or outer covering; (noun) the cast off skin.

Mucus: slime produced by glands on or in an animal.

Nekton: freely swimming inhabitants of the surface and mid-waters in the sea.

Notochord: primitive axial skeletal rod in Chordata (including Vertebrata).

Operculum: lid or flap forming protection, e.g. to shells of snails or barnacles, or over gill-openings of fishes.

Parapodium: paired *lateral* processes carrying hairs or spines, on body segments of bristle-worms.

Parasite: an organism which associates with another (called host) which it exploits for its food (sucking blood, etc.).

Photosynthesis: carbon assimilation in plants, by means of the green colouring matter, *chlorophyll*, in the presence of light.

Plankton: floating or drifting life of surface waters.

Plastron: *ventral* body shield of turtles.

Polyp(e): individual animal of a hydroid or coral colony.

Posterior: backward of; behind; nearer the tail. Opposite of *anterior*.

Proboscis: process jutting out in front of head; snout.

Prop-roots: aerial roots growing downward from stem, as in mangroves.

Radula: horny strip bearing rows of minute teeth found in mouth cavity of snails.

Retractile: capable of being withdrawn.

Rostrum: snout; projecting process between eyes, as in prawns.

Scale: thin, flat, horny plate.

Scute: an external horny or bony plate.

Serrated: with minute, saw-like teeth.

Sessile: attached or stationary.

Seta: bristle-like structure.

Siphon: a tube through which water passes, e.g. into and out of mantle cavity in molluscs.

Spicule: a fine needle-like skeletal structure in sponges and echinoderms.

Swimmerets: paired abdominal *appendages* of crustaceans, functional partly for swimming.

Symbiosis: intimate association between two organisms of different kinds, often to their mutual advantage.

Tentacle: slender flexible organ on head of many *invertebrates*, used for feeling.

Test: stout outer covering to body, sometimes forming a shell (e.g. in sea urchins).

Thallus: body, as apart from the *holdfast*, of seaweeds.

Theca: a structure serving as protective covering for an organ or organism. (Also see *Hydrotheca*.)

Thorax: that part of body between head and *abdomen*.

Ventral: pertaining to the abdominal or lower surface; lower than.

FURTHER READING

POPULAR

The Edge of the Sea, Rachel Carson. Staples Press Ltd., London, 276 pages.

The Sea Shore, C. M. Yonge. Collins, London, 311 pages.

Wonder Creatures of the Sea, A. Hyatt Verrill. D. Appleton-Century Company, New York, 272 pages.

A Naturalist in Indian Seas, A. Alcock. John Murray, London, 328 pages.

Indian Molluscs, James Hornell. The Bombay Natural History Society, Bombay, 96 pages.

TECHNICAL

Field Book of Seashore Life, Roy Waldo Miner. G. P. Putnam's Sons, New York, 888 pages.

The Littoral Fauna of Krusadai Island, ed. the Superintendent, Madras Government Museum. Bulletin of the Madras Government Museum, new series, Natural History Section, Vol. 1, no. 1, 196 pages.

The Fauna and Geography of the Maldive and Laccadive Archipelagoes, J. Stanley Gardiner. Cambridge University Press and Macmillan Co. Ltd., Bombay, Vol. I, 471 pages; Vol. II, 1079 pages.

Marine Crabs of Bombay State, B. F. Chhapgar. Department of Fisheries, Bombay State, 89 pages.

Phycologia Indica (Icones of Indian Marine Algae), K.S. Srinivasan, Botanical Survey of India, Calcutta, Vol. I, 52 pages; Vol. II, 60 pages.

INDEX

Numbers in italics refer to pages on **which plants/animals** are illustrated.

74

75

76